Teeny-Tiny
MOCHIMOCHI

Teeny-Tiny
MOCHIMOCHI

MORE THAN 40 ITTY-BITTY MINIS
TO KNIT, WEAR, AND GIVE

Anna Hrachovec

Photography by Brandi Simons

POTTER
CRAFT

NEW YORK

Published in the United States by Potter Craft, an imprint of the Crown Publishing Group, a division of Random House, Inc., New York.

www.crownpublishing.com
www.pottercraft.com

POTTER CRAFT and colophon is a registered trademark of Random House, Inc.

Cover and interior design by Jane Archer/www.psbella.com

Cover photography by Brandi Simons

Hrachovec, Anna.
 Teeny-tiny mochimochi : more than 40 itty-bitty minis to knit, wear, and give / Anna Hrachovec.
   p. cm.
 ISBN-13: 978-0-8230-2692-0 (pbk.)
 ISBN-10: 0-8230-2692-2 ()
1. Amigurumi--Patterns. 2. Soft toy making. I. Title.
 TT829.H734 2011
 745.592'4--dc22

                2010050987

Printed in China
First Printing, 2011

1 2 3 4 5 6 7 8 9 10 / 18 17 16 15 14 13 12 11

To Bonney, no small source of inspiration

Acknowledgments

Thank you to my husband John, who will always be my first toy tester, editor, and advisor for every project.

I am so grateful for my photographer Brandi, who again did a knockout job with fun and beautiful shots for this book. It's a pleasure to work and play with her in Tulsa. Her husband Mike was also a big help, and if it weren't for Sonnie and Sarah, a few Tiny Monkeys would surely still be lost somewhere under a couch.

Thank you to my parents, my sis Leah, and Dave Simons for their various assistance, including finding the perfect props, and to Sarah Loving, our lovely (and very game) model.

Once again, my testers came through with their brave and tireless efforts to make the patterns in this book as good as can be. Thank you especially to Dorien, Jenna, Joan, Marti, and Rikke.

I am also very thankful for all the gorgeous yarn provided by Rhichard Devrieze at Koigu Wool Designs and Stacey Winklepleck at Knit Picks.

Lastly, many thanks to everyone at Potter Craft, especially Joy Aquilino, for seeing the potential in very small things and making this book happen, and to Linda Hetzer, for her ability to wrestle with text and images and always win.

contents

Preface
Tiny Is the New Huge

It's a scientific fact: Everything is more fun in miniature. From itty-bitty plastic sushi in Tokyo, to teeny-weeny purse dogs on Fifth Avenue, to super-small sliders in LA restaurants, tiny versions of everyday stuff make even grumpy old guys smile. And if those wee little things happen to be knitted toys that you made yourself, well, those old grumps might just giggle with glee.

In July 2009, I had just finished *Knitting Mochimochi*, my first book of knitted toy patterns. It had been an exciting, exhilarating experience, and I was ready for a break. Not a break from knitting—let's not kid ourselves—but a new kind of challenge for Mochimochi Land. On a lark, I decided to come up with as many Tiny Toys as I could in one month. It started with a Tiny Brain on July 1. Mostly composed of a bunched-up I-cord, it was about an inch long. As soon as I posted the photo on my blog and saw the enthusiastic comments left by my readers, I knew I had discovered a new obsession. I ended up knitting twenty-three Tiny Things that month, one for every weekday, including a box of tissues, a panda (with an even tinier bamboo shoot), and a melting glacier.

All of these Tiny Things are three-dimensional animals, objects, or people, and they all have that Mochimochi Land anthropomorphism. Why? Because the only thing cuter than a mini knitted forest is a mini knitted forest with twenty-eight little eyes looking back at you!

When my crazy Month of Tiny ended, I was still on a roll, so I continued the Tiny Challenge on a weekly basis. As of this writing, I've kept up my self-imposed Tiny Toys Challenge for over a year, making more than seventy Tinys, and I'm still going. Maybe I will knit a cute tiny coffin on my deathbed.

This book includes patterns for some of my favorite Tiny Things from that fateful July, plus many others, including a bunch that are making their debut in *Teeny-Tiny Mochimochi*. These minuscule creations are deceptively simple to knit using basic techniques, but the results are so magical that friends will think you've got a team of miniature knitting elves at your disposal. And while the Tinys are pretty charming on their own, with a little ingenuity, they can be turned into pins, magnets, Christmas ornaments—anything that could use some scale-model silliness. So pick up your sock yarn and size 1 needles, and make the grouch in your life giggle like a schoolgirl!

Why Tiny?

Nobody needs a reason to knit Tiny Things—it's just fun—but some of us more cautious, left-brained types like to have a little extra justification before we jump into a new project. So here's why it makes sense to go Tiny.

TIME IS MONEY As much as we love knitting, sometimes any project bigger than a single mitten feels like too much of a commitment. Here you can finish an entire project in less than an hour—and it's not a boring swatch, but a sweet little creature! Tinys are some of the fastest projects that will ever fly off your needles.

MONEY IS MONEY No need to break the bank for these guys! If you've ever knitted a pair of socks, you probably already have enough yarn left over to make more than a few Tiny Toys. Or, you can pick up a skein or two of any fingering-weight yarn and then make dozens (yup, dozens!) of them. It's all in the magic of yardage.

YOUR GIFT LIST IS ANYTHING BUT TINY Friends, coworkers, parents, kids, teachers, siblings, significant others, not-so-significant others—your list is long. You could pick up 20 gift cards (kind of impersonal), or buy a case of scented candles (kind of smelly), or you could try to knit 20 hats by December (don't forget to take everyone's measurements). Or you could create Tiny Toys that you can make from one skein of yarn in about an hour each. Check out "Tiny Possibilities" on pages 132–135 for some fun ideas.

IT'S NOT AS HARD AS IT LOOKS As intimidating as miniature projects might look, they use very simple techniques. If you can finish knitting a hat using double-pointed needles, you're more than ready to tackle a Tiny. Check out the techniques for toy knitting on pages 14–28 and, if you need a refresher, the basic knitting techniques on pages 136–140.

How Tiny?

Tiny Ingredients

Now that you have caught the Tiny bug (it's highly contagious, so you never really had a chance), let's talk about what you need to get started on making some Tinys of your own.

Yarn

Unlike a sock or a sweater, Tinys don't have to be sized just right to fit someone. That means you can make them with just about any kind of yarn you like. That said, what makes Tinys so adorably tiny is the fingering-weight yarn that I use, the same yarn used to knit socks. It's thin and sturdy and comes in lots of colors. I prefer to work with yarn made of wool or a wool blend—it feels nice and is easy to work with—but you can also use cotton or acrylic yarn, especially if that's what you have on hand.

Try making a Tiny with the extra yarn you have from a previous project and see how you like it. If you're hooked, run to your local yarn store and pick up some fingering-weight sock yarn. You'll be amazed at how many Tinys you can make from just one skein.

Needles

Tinys are knitted in the round, which makes them three-dimensional and mostly seamless. This circular knitting is done with double-pointed needles (or dpns for short), which come in sets of five needles, but are usually used just four at a time. The small knitting circumference that you can get with double-pointed needles is a must for Tiny knitting. You can also use two double-pointed needles to knit flat pieces, so they can do double duty.

The size of your needles will depend on the weight of the yarn you use. I used size 1 U.S. (2.25mm) needles for all of the projects in this book, but you may want to go up or down slightly in size, depending on the type of yarn that you are working with and how tightly you knit. As a general rule, use a needle that is one or two sizes smaller than the recommended needle size for a particular yarn so you'll have a tight fabric without gaps that the stuffing can show through.

Double-pointed needles come in a variety of materials, including wood, bamboo, metal, and plastic. Individual tastes vary, and many local yarn stores will let you try out a few different types of needles before buying, so you can find what you feel most comfortable with. My own favorite is bamboo—it's lightweight and strong, with a smooth, but not slippery, surface.

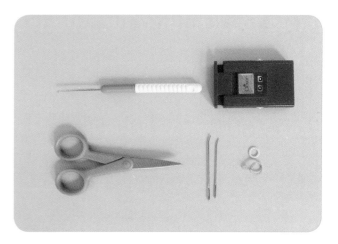

Stuffing

You'll put lots of love inside of your Tinys, but you need to put in something soft and fluffy, too. There are many types of stuffing available. I prefer polyester fiberfill because, for some Tinys, you will have to weave a knitted I-cord all the way through the stuffed piece, and slippery polyester will allow it to go through smoothly. In a pinch, you can use yarn scraps to stuff your Tinys.

A note About Gauge

Checking gauge is absolutely necessary when you're planning to knit a garment or other project in which measurements are important. Because toys don't need to fit a particular size, I recommend not checking gauge at all—it's more fun to just get started.

A note About Yardage

The patterns in this book do not include yardage. This is because the yardage needed of any given color of yarn is very small—usually 7 yards (6.4m) or less. You will never need more than one skein of yarn for any project.

Tools

Scissors are a must, and because the projects in this book are so small, you'll need a small pair with a pointed tip.

A tapestry needle looks like a jumbo-sized sewing needle. It's used with yarn for seaming, embroidering details, and weaving in loose ends.

A stitch marker helps you remember where the rounds in your knitting begin and end. You can buy small plastic rings, but for tiny toys I prefer to just tie a small piece of contrasting-colored yarn in a loop.

A crochet hook is used for attaching hair to a toy or to pick up stitches dropped accidentally. Use one the same size as the knitting needles you are using.

A counter helps you keep track of the row or round you're on; the type pictured is an easy-to-use clicking device. Or you can simply make hash marks on a piece of paper.

Straight pins are helpful when attaching pieces together so you can get the spacing right before you sew them in place.

Safety pins make handy stitch holders for tiny projects. Sometimes you'll use them to hold live stitches temporarily so you can come back to them later.

Basic Toy Knitting Techniques

If you are a beginning knitter, or if you would like to brush up on the basics, you can refer to the Knitting Essentials on pages 136-140.

Using Double-Pointed Needles

Double-pointed needles allow you to knit three-dimensional pieces in varying sizes and shapes, so they are perfect for knitting tiny toys. Don't let all those points frighten you—like straight knitting, you're always working with only two needles at a time, letting the other needles simply hold your stitches until you come around to them.

1 Begin by casting all your stitches onto one needle. Then distribute the stitches evenly onto 3 needles, slipping the stitches purlwise so they don't get twisted. Hold the needle with the yarn attached in your right hand. To make sure that you aren't twisting the stitches, align the cast-on edge to the insides of the needles.

2 Use a fourth needle to knit the stitches on the needle in your left hand. Be sure to pull the working yarn tightly for the first stitch, so that you complete a circle without a big gap.

3 When you finish knitting the stitches from the needle in your left hand, the stitches will all end up on the right (fourth) needle. Slide them down a bit on the right needle so they won't slip off. Then continue knitting the stitches on the next needle to the left onto your now-empty needle.

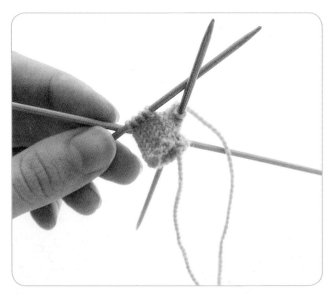

4 Continue knitting from the needle in your left hand to the fourth needle in your right, shifting the needles around in a circle as you go. When you reach the end of one round, just continue knitting from the next needle to continue to the next round. If you keep knitting this way, you will see a three-dimensional shape begin to form.

Using a Stitch Marker

A stitch marker helps you keep track of where the rounds begin. You can make one yourself by tying a piece of contrasting-colored yarn into a loop.

 At the beginning of a round, place the marker on the right needle, adjacent to the stitch with the yarn attached.

 For the first stitch in the first round (or the next round, if you are placing the marker in an in-progress piece), knit the stitch directly onto the needle with the marker on it. This will prevent the marker from falling off the needle.

 Use a fourth needle to knit the second stitch in the round, as you normally would, and continue knitting as usual for the rest of the round. When you come to the stitch marker at the end of the round, simply slip it onto the needle in your right hand, and continue on to the next round.

Beginning with a Small Number of Stitches

Many Tiny patterns start off with only four stitches on the needles, which are increased to eight stitches after the first round to make a flat circular shape. Instead of placing the first four stitches onto three needles, it's much easier to knit the first round as you would an I-cord. (You can also use this technique for the first round in patterns that call for a six-stitch cast-on, if you find it more comfortable than beginning with six stitches on three needles.)

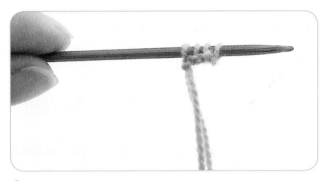

 After casting on, leave the stitches on one double-pointed needle, and slide the end that does not have the yarn attached to the right side of the needle.

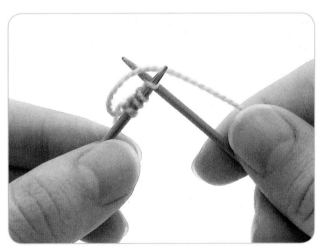

 Bring the working yarn around the back of the stitches, and, pulling tightly on the yarn, knit onto a second needle. (In most cases, you will work a kfb increase [page 138].)

Continued on the next page.

3 Once you have finished knitting the stitches on the needle and have increased the total number of stitches, distribute the stitches onto 3 double-pointed needles and continue knitting in the round.

2 When you are finished knitting and are ready to close up the piece, cut the yarn, leaving a tail of a few inches, and thread the end onto a tapestry needle. Beginning with the first stitch in the round, thread the tapestry needle purlwise through each of the stitches in order in the round, slipping the stitches off the double-pointed needles as you go.

Closing Up

Before you close up, you will usually need to stuff the piece. Then you will break the yarn and draw it tightly through the live stitches to finish off.

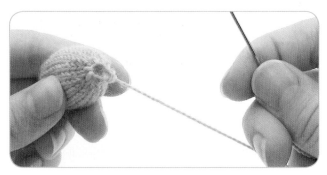

3 Pull the end of the cut yarn tightly to draw the stitches closed.

1 First, stuff the piece—usually this is done before you make the last decrease round, so that there is room for you to poke the stuffing inside with your finger.

4 To secure the stitches, insert the tapestry needle into the hole that you just closed up and weave the loose end through the piece.

Weaving in Loose Ends

After knitting, stuffing, and seaming, you will probably have some loose ends of yarn that need to be tidied up.

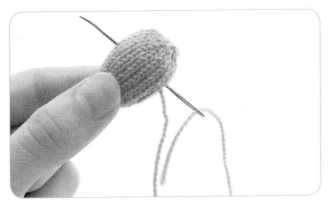

1 Thread the loose end onto a tapestry needle. Insert the needle back through the toy and all the way out the other side. To make sure that the loose end won't work its way back out, weave it in and out of the toy once or twice more to secure it—be careful not to pull too tightly, or you'll end up with lumpy spots where the yarn is pulling on the fabric and stuffing.

2 When the loose end is sufficiently woven in, cut the yarn short, pressing on the piece gently so the end will be hidden inside the toy.

Tiny Techniques and Tips

Knitting teeny-tiny toys is similar to knitting regular-sized toys—but with tinier details and fewer small pieces to assemble. Many of the Tinys consist of a simple body piece that you will embellish with simple features and simple appendages to turn it into a simply adorable creature. Here are some techniques and tricks that will make these projects fun and quick.

Embroidering Features

For most tiny toys, I suggest adding eyes to the body before any other parts. Then the eyes can act as a guide for where to attach everything else.

Because the projects are so tiny, so are the eyes. They are usually just two small stitches made with black yarn, either spanning the length of one knitted stitch or one half (one "leg") of a stitch.

① Thread a piece of black yarn onto a small tapestry needle. Once you have chosen the placement of an eye, stick the needle in one side of the body, and bring it out at the place where you want the eye to go. Pull most of the yarn through, leaving a tail sticking out on the other side.

② Make the first stitch of the eye, and bring the needle out in the same place that you began the stitch. You are essentially "wrapping" the knitted stitch with the contrasting color.

③ Make another stitch, identical to the first. To make the second eye, bring the needle out a few stitches away from the first eye. Then repeat Step 2.

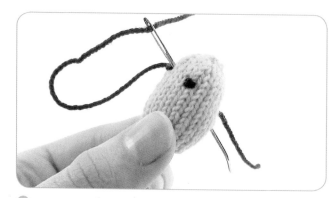

④ When you make the last eye stitch for this creature, bring the needle back out on the other side of the body.

5 Weave in the loose ends by inserting the tapestry needle into the same place where the ends emerge from the body, and again bringing the needle out on the other side of the body. This method of weaving in the loose stitch will prevent a stray stitch in the contrasting color, and the yarn will catch on the stuffing, making it secure.

6 After weaving the loose ends, pull gently on each end and cut it close to the body so it will be hidden.

Embroidery Tips

Embroider eyes with horizontal stitches when the body is vertically oriented.

Embroider eyes with vertical stitches when the body is horizontally oriented.

For a more three-dimensional look, in the same color or with a contrasting color, wrap the knitted stitch or stitches multiple times until there is a visible bump.

Picking Up Stitches For Appendages

Rather than making separate pieces for appendages and sewing them on, the patterns in this book call for stitches to be picked up from the body and then worked either as an I-cord or a flat piece to become ears, arms, or other parts.

Picking up stitches from the middle of a knitted piece is similar to the way you would pick up stitches on an edge. One difference is that the orientation of your piece matters when you pick up stitches to knit them flat, as in a wing or an ear: The side closest to you when you pick up the stitches will be the smoother knit side.

❶ After choosing the placement and orientation of the stitches you will pick up, slip a needle under the first stitch, and wrap the yarn around the needle as if to knit.

❷ Pull the yarn through from under the stitch as you would a regular knitted stitch.

If you'll be working back and forth after picking up stitches, turn the piece around to purl the next row.

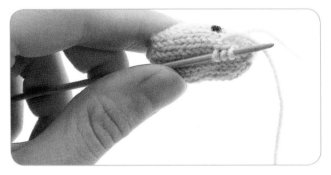

If you'll be working an I-cord after picking up stitches, slide the stitches down to the right end of the needle.

Tips on Picking Up Stitches

You will always pick up stitches from right to left. That means when you are making symmetrical appendages, you will begin picking up from opposite directions.

When picking up stitches for a left ear, begin near the top of the head and work your way down the side of the head.

I-Cord Appendages

Another simple way to make appendages, especially those that are thin and long, is to make one long I-cord that can become two arms or two legs by inserting it through the body and letting both ends stick out.

2 Insert the needle into the body piece at the point at which you want one arm or leg to be attached, and bring the needle out where you want the other appendage to be attached. Make sure that the needle is going in and out between knitted stitches, not splitting the yarn.

1 After you finish making the I-cord as the pattern instructs, thread the tail end you used to close off the final stitches through a tapestry needle.

3 Pull the I-cord through the body, so that an equal length sticks out on each side. If you have some difficulty getting the I-cord to come out the other side, this means that either it is getting caught in the stuffing or you split the yarn on the body with the needle and you are trying to pull the I-cord through a strand of yarn. Pull the needle out and try again.

Continued on the next page.

When picking up stitches for a right ear, begin at the side of the head and work your way toward the top of the head.

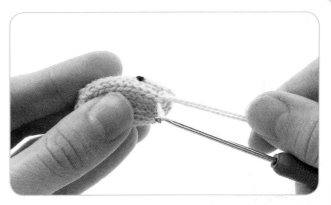

If you find it difficult to pick up the stitches by wrapping a needle, use a small crochet hook. When using a hook, you can either slip each stitch onto a knitting needle after you pick it up, or pick them all up in a row on the hook and then transfer them all onto a knitting needle.

4 Once you are happy with the placement and lengths of the appendages, weave in the ends of the I-cord. Insert the tapestry needle back into the I-cord, and weave it through the I-cord and through the body. Because the I-cord is very skinny, you may need to go in and out of it a few times with the needle, but these stitches will be invisible, so don't worry about making it perfect.

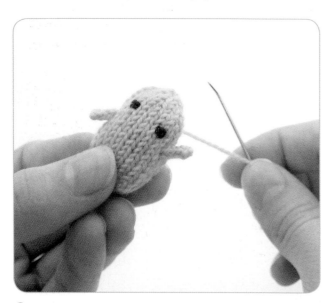

5 These I-cord appendages are very poseable as you weave in the ends, so if you want your little guy to have his arms pointing up or down or sideways, now is your chance!

Joined Legs

Another way to make tiny appendages is to work them seamlessly by joining them in the round, a method particularly useful for legs. The two techniques shown here have different steps, depending on how many stitches each leg comprises.

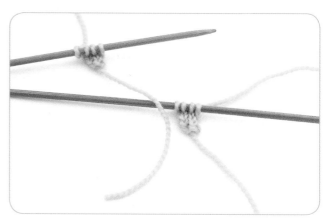

Begin by making one I-cord leg as specified in the pattern (either a 3-stitch or 4-stitch I-cord), then break the yarn and set the live stitches aside on a spare needle. Make a second leg in the same way as the first, but without breaking the yarn. See below for the next step for 3-stitch legs; see next page for the next step for 4-stitch legs.

THREE-STITCH LEGS

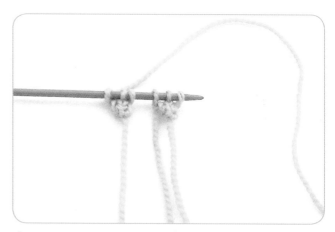

1 After beginning the legs (above), for 3-stitch legs, place the live stitches of both legs side by side on one needle, situated so that the working yarn is attached to the leftmost stitch. Slide the stitches to the right end of the needle.

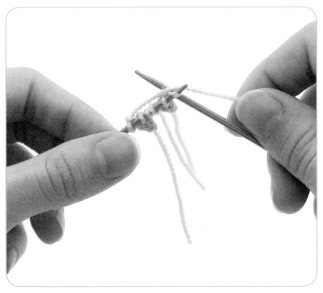

2 Bring the yarn from around the back of the legs, pulling on it tightly, to knit the first stitch I-cord style. Continue to knit all six stitches onto the needle in your right hand. After you have finished knitting this round, distribute the stitches onto 3 needles, and continue to knit them in a round.

FOUR-STITCH LEGS

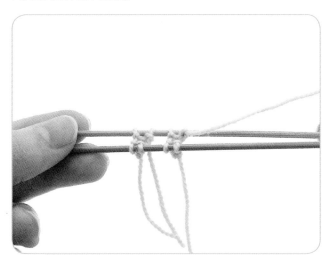

1 After beginning the legs (page 22, top right), for 4-stitch legs, place the live stitches of each leg onto 2 needles, with the first 2 stitches of each leg side by side on one needle and the last 2 stitches of each leg side by side on the other needle. Hold the needles parallel to each other, with the working yarn attached to the rightmost stitch on the back needle.

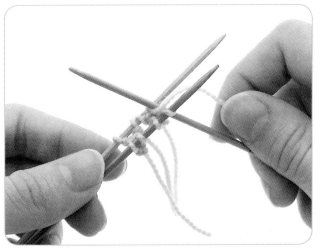

2 With a third needle, knit one round, beginning with the needle in front, then flipping the needles around to continue on to the back needle. After you have finished knitting this round, distribute the stitches onto 3 needles, and continue to knit them in a round.

Stuffing

Just a little stuffing goes a long way when working with small pieces—you'll usually need just a pinch. If your fingers aren't doing the trick, use the tip of a closed pair of small scissors—the metal really seems to grab onto the stuffing.

Additional Toy Techniques

Here are a few more techniques you'll need from time to time. You'll find them helpful when knitting toys of any size.

Seaming

MATTRESS STITCH

Most of the patterns in this book don't require you to sew pieces together, but sometimes a little seaming is necessary to get the right shape and structure. Beautiful seaming is easy with mattress stitch.

Mattress stitch is a technique that allows you to sew pieces together on the right sides for an almost invisible seam. There are a few variations on the simple technique, but once you understand the basics you'll see how they can be combined for all sorts of seaming. To make it easy to understand, it is shown here with flat pieces and contrasting-colored yarn.

VERTICAL MATTRESS STITCH

Use this variation when you are seaming two pieces together with the vertical rows of stitches lining up.

1 On one piece, locate the first stitch on the edge of the piece, and slip the tapestry needle under the horizontal bar that appears between this stitch and the next one in from the edge. Pull the yarn through.

2 Slip the needle under the corresponding bar on the second piece.

3 Go back to the first piece, and slip the needle under the next bar up. Go back and forth in this way a few times.

4 When you pull the yarn tightly, the seam will disappear. Continue stitching the rest of the seam.

HORIZONTAL MATTRESS STITCH

Use this variation when you are seaming cast-on or bound-off edges together, or whenever two horizontal rows of stitches line up.

1 Slip the needle under the point of the V on the first stitch on the edge of one piece, and pull the yarn through.

2 Slip the needle under the point of the corresponding V on the other piece.

3 Go back and forth in this way along the seam.

4 Pull the yarn tightly and the seam will disappear.

HORIZONTAL-TO-VERTICAL MATTRESS STITCH

To seam together two pieces whose stitches run in opposite directions, you will combine the vertical and horizontal mattress stitch.

1 Slip the needle under the bar on the vertical piece and under the V on the horizontal piece. Continue to go back and forth in this way along the seam.

2 Because knitted stitches are slightly wider than they are tall, your total number of bars and Vs won't match up exactly. Compensate for this difference by slipping the needle under 2 bars instead of just one every few stitches.

PERPENDICULAR MATTRESS STITCH

Most of the mattress stitch seaming for tiny toys will be attaching three-dimensional pieces rather than flat pieces. On these occasions, use a combination of the previous techniques for perpendicular mattress stitch.

1 To attach two 3-dimensional pieces together, locate the place where you want them to be joined, and pin or hold them in place.

3 For the next stitch on the larger piece, slip the needle diagonally down through the side of one knitted stitch and up through the middle of the stitch below it and to the left.

2 Note that at the top and bottom, the stitches on the smaller piece line up horizontally with the stitches on the large piece. Beginning at the top, use horizontal mattress stitch until the stitches no longer line up.

4 Now switch to vertical-to-horizontal mattress stitch, slipping the needle under the bars on the larger piece and the Vs on the smaller piece.

5 When the stitches stop lining up vertical-to-horizontal, again make one or more diagonal stitches on the larger piece, then switch back to horizontal mattress stitch for the bottom of the smaller piece. Continue to seam in a circle in this way until you come back to the place where you started. The result is a seamless joining, with the smaller piece sticking straight out from the larger one.

BACK STITCH

Back stitch is another seaming technique that you can use to attach a flat piece to a three-dimensional piece. This simple stitching technique creates a secure seam. Working back stitch in a contrasting color creates an embroidered line.

2 Insert the needle back down in the same place that you inserted it in Step 1, so that the second stitch abuts the first. Again, bring the needle back up at a distance equal to the length of one stitch.

1 Overlap the 2 pieces you want to attach. Insert the tapestry needle straight down through both pieces, and bring it back up some distance away. Make the stitches the same length on top and underneath.

3 Repeat Step 2 across the seam.

Using a Crochet Hook to Attach Hair

Here's a simple way to give your Tiny a full mop on top. You'll need is a crochet hook (more or less the same size as your knitting needles) and a pair of scissors.

① Cut about a 5" strand of contrasting yarn. Insert the crochet hook under a bar that appears between 2 stitches on the main piece, and hook the folded strand of contrasting yarn onto it.

② Draw the crochet hook out from under the bar on the main piece, pulling the contrasting yarn partway out with it.

③ Remove the crochet hook from the loop of contrasting yarn, and insert the 2 tail ends through the loop. Pull to tighten the knot.

④ To make the resulting knot less visible, poke it down into the main piece using a closed pair of scissors. Then trim the 2 strands of yarn to the desired length.

Cleaning and Care

If your Tinys are used as accessories, they might need a little sprucing up now and then to keep looking their best. Wash them gently by hand and air-dry them. By hand is best; they might get lost in the washing machine! If pieces become loose through wear and tear, repair them with just a few small reinforcing stitches.

Not So Tiny Toys

Miniature knitted toys aren't a good match for small kiddos, but you can certainly scale the patterns up to be more kid-friendly. Simply grab a chunky-weight yarn and bigger needles, and follow the pattern as written.

To make this Jumbo Easter Bunny, which is 3½" tall, I used Cascade 128 yarn (5/bulky; 100% wool; 3½ oz/100g, 128 yds/117m) and a set of size 7 U.S. (4.5mm) double-pointed needles.

Not for Tiny Tots

If you use the recommended yarn to knit the toys in this book, most of them will measure between 1" and 3" in length. Can we say choking hazard? Best not to risk it, so be sure to keep your Tinys away from small children under the age of three years.

How Tiny Can You Go?

If you have the opposite inclination and want to make your Tiny as itty-bitty, teeny-weeny as possible, scale the pattern down with lace-weight yarn and super-thin needles.

To make this Micro Easter Bunny, which is just under an inch tall, I used Knit Picks Shadow Tonal Lace Yarn (0/lace; 100% wool; 1¾ oz/50g, 440 yds/402m) and size 0000 (1.25mm) double-pointed needles. Now that's tiny!

Tiny Animals

Tiny Chickens

These little cluckers were feeling proud of their big accomplishments a few hours ago, but now they're just trying to figure out how to get off this ride. . . .

SPECIAL TECHNIQUES
Picking up stitches (page 20)

YARN
Fingering-weight yarn in 3 colors and black
Samples made with Knit Picks Palette
(1/super fine; 100% wool; 1 3/4 oz/50g, 231 yd/211m)
Color 1 (body): 23730 (Cream), 24240 (Doe)
Color 2 (beak and feet): 24250 (Semolina)
Color 3 (comb): 24553 (Serrano)
Black: 23729

OTHER SUPPLIES
Set of size 1 U.S. (2.25mm) double-pointed needles
Small tapestry needle
Stuffing

Tiny Chickens are about 1" tall, or 15 times tinier than an Ameraucana chicken.

BODY *(worked bottom to top)*
With Color 1, CO 6 sts onto 3 needles and join in a round.
Rnd 1: [Kfb] 6 times (12 sts).
Rnd 2: [Kfb, k1] 6 times (18 sts).
Rnd 3: Knit.
Rnd 4: [Kfb, k2] 6 times (24 sts).
Rnds 5–8: Knit (4 rnds).
Rnd 9: [K2tog, k2] 6 times (18 sts).
Rnd 10: [K2tog, k1] 6 times (12 sts).
Rnds 11–14: Knit (4 rnds).
Stuff the piece.

Rnd 15: [K2tog] 6 times (6 sts).
Break the yarn and draw it tightly through the sts with a tapestry needle.

FEATURES
For beak, wrap one stitch 3 times with Color 2, placed about 4 sts from the top of the head.
For eyes, make 2 sts with Black for each, placed about 2 sts apart.

COMB
With Color 3, pick up and knit 3 sts at the top of the head (Ⓐ, above, right). Turn, and bind off the sts.
Note: You will probably end up with a row of Color 3 sts on one side of the head. To make the coloring more even, weave in the loose ends of Color 3 so that they cover the gaps.

Ⓐ To make the comb, pick up and knit 3 stitches at the top of the head, then turn and bind off the stitches.

WINGS (make 2)

Flip the chicken upside down, and with Color 1, pick up and knit 4 sts at the side of the Body, just under the first decrease round (B , below).

B To begin making a wing, turn the Body upside down and pick up and knit 4 stitches horizontally at the side of the Body, just under the first decrease round. Turn piece.

Row 1: Purl.
Row 2: Knit.

Break the yarn, and pulling across the purl side of piece, draw it tightly through the sts with a tapestry needle.

You can either tack the wing down onto the Body with the loose end, or weave the end back through the wing for outstretched wings.

LEGS

With Color 2, CO 2 sts onto one needle.

Knit 12 rows of I-cord, then break the yarn and draw it tightly through the sts with a tapestry needle.

With the end still threaded on the tapestry needle, thread the I-cord through the bottom front side of the Body, going in and coming out at the second increase round, and spaced about 5 sts apart. Pull the I-cord halfway through the Body, so that an even amount sticks out from each side. When you weave in the loose ends, bend the ends of the I-cord upward and tack them in place for feet.

FINISHING

Weave in loose ends.

Tiny Monkeys

Tiny Monkeys are more fun than . . . themselves!

SPECIAL TECHNIQUES
Picking up stitches (page 20)

YARN
Fingering-weight yarn in 3 colors and black
Samples made with Knit Picks Palette
(1/super fine; 100% wool; 1¾ oz/50g, 231 yd/211m)
Color 1 (body): 23724 (Sky), 23723 (Pool), 23722
(Blue)
Color 2 (banana): 24250 (Semolina)

Color 3 (banana tip): 24562 (Bison)
Black: 23729

OTHER SUPPLIES
Set of size 1 U.S. (2.25mm) double-pointed needles
Small tapestry needle
Stuffing

Tiny Monkeys are about 1" tall, or 8 times tinier than a Chiquita banana.

BODY *(worked bottom to top)*

With Color 1, CO 6 sts onto 3 needles and join in a round.

Rnd 1: [Kfb] 6 times (12 sts).

Rnd 2: [Kfb, k1] 6 times (18 sts).

Rnds 3–14: Knit (12 rnds).

Rnd 15: [K2tog, k1] 6 times (12 sts).

Stuff the piece.

Rnd 16: [K2tog] 6 times (6 sts).

Break the yarn and draw it tightly through the sts using a tapestry needle.

FEATURES

With Black, embroider eyes using 2 sts for each, spaced about 3 sts apart.

Embroider the nose with one longer stitch of Color 3.

EARS *(make 2)*

Turn the Body so the monkey is horizontal, with the eyes facing up, and with Color 1, pick up and knit 4 sts at the side of the head, placed about 3 sts from the top of the head.

To begin making an ear, turn the Body so that it is horizontal, with the eyes facing up, and pick up and knit 4 stitches at the side of the head.

After picking up the sts, turn to work them straight.

Row 1: Purl.
Row 2: Knit.

Break the yarn, and pulling it across the purl side of the piece, draw it tightly through the sts with a tapestry needle.

ARMS

With Color 1, CO 2 sts onto one needle.

Knit 18 rows of I-cord, then break the yarn and draw it tightly through the sts with a tapestry needle.

With the end still threaded on the tapestry needle, insert the I-cord through the sides of the Body, going in and coming out at about 2 sts below and just to the inside of the ears. Pull the I-cord halfway through the Body, so that an even amount sticks out from each side. Weave the loose ends back through the I-cord and the Body.

LEGS

With Color 1, CO 2 sts onto one needle.

Knit 14 rows of I-cord, then break the yarn and draw it tightly through the sts with a tapestry needle.

With the end still threaded on the tapestry needle, insert the I-cord through the Body, going in and coming out at the last increase round, and spaced about 4 sts apart. Pull the I-cord halfway through the Body, so that an even amount sticks out from each side. Weave the loose ends back through the Legs and Body.

TAIL

With Color 1, pick up and knit 2 sts at the back of the Body on the last increase round.

Knit 12 rows of I-cord, then break the yarn and draw it tightly through the sts with a tapestry needle.

Weave the loose end back through the Tail and Body.

BANANA

With Color 2, CO 4 sts onto one needle.

Knit 4 rows of I-cord, then break the yarn and draw it tightly through the sts with a tapestry needle.

Weave in the loose ends, and use one end to attach to the Monkey's yarn. With Color 3, embroider a few sts onto the top of the Banana.

FINISHING

Weave in loose ends.

Tiny Elephant

Tiny Elephant wants . . . this . . . peanut! All she has to do is figure out how to crack it.

SPECIAL TECHNIQUES
Picking up stitches (page 20)

YARN
Fingering-weight yarn in one color and black
Samples made with Koigu Premium Merino
(1/super fine; 100% wool; 1¾ oz/50g, 170 yd/155m)

Main Color (MC): 2392 (gray), 1150.5 (light pink),
or 2300 (light blue)
Black: 2400

OTHER SUPPLIES
Set of size 1 U.S. (2.25mm) double-pointed needles
Small tapestry needle
Stuffing

> **Tiny Elephant is about 1" tall, or 132 times tinier than an African elephant.**

BODY
With MC, CO 6 sts onto 3 needles
and join in a round.
Rnd 1: [Kfb] 6 times (12 sts).
Rnd 2: [Kfb, k1] 6 times (18 sts).
Rnd 3: Knit.
Rnd 4: [Kfb, k2] 6 times (24 sts).
Rnds 5–12: Knit (8 rounds).
Rnd 13: [K2tog, k2] 6 times (18 sts).
Rnd 14: Knit.
Rnd 15: [K2tog, k1] 6 times (12 sts).
  Stuff the piece.
Rnd 16: [K2tog] 6 times (6 sts).
  Place the sts onto one needle to
work the next row as an I-cord.

Rnd 17: [K2tog] 3 times (3 sts).
  Knit 4 rows of I-cord, then break
the yarn and draw it tightly through
the sts with a tapestry needle.

EYES
With Black, embroider eyes with 2
sts for each, placed about 5 sts back
from the trunk and spaced about 6
sts apart.

EARS (make 2)
Turn the Body so trunk faces away
from you, and pick up and knit 5 sts in a
row, placed about 2 sts behind an eye.
  Turn and purl 5 sts.
Next row: K2tog, k1, k2tog (3 sts).
  BO on the purl side.

FEET (make 4)
Pick up and knit 3 sts at the bottom
of the Body.
  Knit 2 rows of I-cord, then break the
yarn and draw it tightly through the sts.

TAIL
Pick up and knit 2 sts at the back of the
Body, just above the cast-on sts.
  Work 4 rows of I-cord, then break the
yarn and draw it tightly through the sts.
  Cut 2 strands of yarn and thread
them through the end of the Tail. Tie
each in a tight knot and trim.
  Weave in loose ends.

To make an ear, turn the Body so that the trunk
faces away from you, and pick up and knit 5
stitches in a row, placed 2 stitches behind an eye.

Tiny Fish

His dream is to win a dance competition, but his performances are always flops—literally.

SPECIAL TECHNIQUES
Kitchener stitch (page 140)
Picking up stitches (page 20)

YARN
Fingering-weight yarn in 3 colors and black
Sample made with Koigu Premium Merino
(1/super fine; 100% wool; 1¾ oz/50g, 170 yd/155m)
Color 1 (body): 1200

Color 2 (bubbles): 2130
Color 3 (string): 0000
Black: 2400

OTHER SUPPLIES
Set of size 1 U.S. (2.25mm) double-pointed needles
Small tapestry needle
Stuffing

Tiny Fish is about 1" long, or 23 times tinier than a large goldfish.

BODY

With Color 1, CO 6 sts onto 3 needles, and join in a round.
Rnd 1: [Kfb] 6 times (12 sts).
Rnd 2: Knit.
Rnd 3: [M1, k2] 6 times (18 sts).
Rnd 4: Knit.
Rnd 5: [M1, k3] 6 times (24 sts).
Rnds 6–8: Knit.
Rnd 9: [K2tog, k2] 6 times (18 sts).
Rnd 10: Knit.
Rnd 11: [K2tog, k1] 6 times (12 sts).
Rnd 12: [K2tog] 6 times (6 sts).
Stuff the piece.
Rnd 13: [M1, k1] 6 times (12 sts).
Rnd 14: Knit.
  Divide the sts onto 2 needles, with 6 sts on each needle, and bind off using kitchener stitch.

EYES

With Black, embroider eyes using 2 sts for each, placed about 3 sts from the closed up end of the Body and spaced about 6 sts apart.

FINS (make 2)

  Flip the Body upside down, and with Color 1, pick up and knit 4 sts at the side of the Body, placed about 3 sts back from the eye.
  Turn and purl, then break the yarn and draw it tightly through the sts with a tapestry needle.
  With the end still threaded on the tapestry needle, tack down at the side of the Body.

BUBBLES (make 3)

With Color 2, CO 6 sts onto 3 needles and join in a round.
Rnd 1: [Kfb] 6 times (12 sts).
Rnds 2 and 3: Knit.
Rnd 4: [K2tog] 6 times
  Insert a very small amount of stuffing into the piece. Break the yarn and draw it tightly through the sts with a tapestry needle.

FINISHING

Cut an approximately 8"-long strand of Color 3, and use a tapestry needle to thread the Bubbles onto the yarn. Thread the fish on at the end, and make a few sts into the Body to secure in place.
  Tie a knot at the top to hang.

To begin a fin, flip the Body upside down, and pick up and knit 4 stitches horizontally on one side of the Body, placed 3 stitches back from the eye.

Tiny Dinosaur

When dinosaurs roamed the earth, this guy scampered around the earth.

SPECIAL TECHNIQUES
Picking up stitches (page 20)

YARN
Fingering-weight yarn in 2 colors and black
Sample made with Koigu Premium Merino
(1/super fine; 100% wool; 1¾ oz/50g, 170 yd/155m)
Main Color (MC): 1520

Contrasting Color (CC): 2100
Black: 2400

OTHER SUPPLIES
Set of size 1 U.S. (2.25mm) double-pointed needles
Small tapestry needle
Stuffing

> Tiny Dinosaur is about 1" long, or 64 times tinier than the largest dinosaur fossil ever found.

BODY

With MC, CO 4 sts onto one needle.
Knit 7 rows of I-cord.
Row 8 (work as I-cord): K1, [kfb] twice, k1 (6 sts).

Distribute the sts onto 3 needles to work in a round.
Rnd 9: Knit.
Rnd 10: K1, [kfb] 4 times, k1 (10 sts).
Rnd 11: Knit.
Rnd 12: k1, [Kfb] 8 times, k1 (18 sts).
Rnds 13–19: Knit (7 rounds).
Rnd 20: [K2tog, k1] 6 times (12 sts).
Stuff the piece.
Rnd 21: [K2tog] 6 times (6 sts).

Break the yarn and draw it tightly through the sts with a tapestry needle.

EYES

With Black, embroider the eyes on the top (curved) side of the Body, using 2 sts for each, placed about 2 sts from the closed up end of the Body and about 5 sts apart.

FEET *(make 4)*

With MC, pick up and knit 3 sts: for the front feet, just under and behind the eyes on the bottom side of the Body, and for the back feet, just in front of the I-cord tail on the bottom side of the Body.

Knit 2 rows of I-cord, then break the yarn and draw it tightly through the sts with a tapestry needle. Weave in loose ends.

SPIKES

With CC, embroider a line of sts going down the dinosaur's back and tail. Make bigger sts on the Body spaced more widely, and make smaller, closer-together sts on the tail. Go back over this row of sts once more to make the spikes thicker.

To make spikes, embroider a line of stitches down the dino's back and tail, then go back over the stitches to thicken them.

FINISHING

Weave in loose ends.

Tiny Lions

They both want to be King of the Jungle someday, but for now they're co-captains of a potted fern.

YARN

Fingering-weight yarn in 2 colors and black
Samples made with Koigu Premium Merino
(1/super fine; 100% wool; 1¾ oz/50g, 170 yd/155m)
Main Color (MC): 2100
Contrasting Color (CC): 1200 (orange-yellow),
2395 (brown), Black: 2400

OTHER SUPPLIES

Set of size 1 U.S. (2.25mm) double-pointed needles
Set of size 6 U.S. (4mm) double-pointed needles
(for mane)
Small tapestry needle
Stuffing

Tiny Lions are about 1" long, or 240 times tinier than a lion in London's Trafalgar Square.

BODY (worked back to front)

With MC, CO 6 sts onto 3 needles and join in a round.

Rnd 1: [Kfb] 6 times (12 sts).
Rnd 2: Knit.
Rnd 3: [Kfb, k1] 6 times (18 sts).
Rnd 4: Knit.
Rnd 5: [Kfb, k2] 6 times (24 sts).
Rnds 6–11: Knit (6 rounds).
Rnd 12: [K2tog, k2] 6 times (18 sts).
Rnd 13: Knit.
Rnd 14: [K2tog, k1] 6 times (12 sts).
  Stuff the piece.
Rnd 15: [K2tog] 6 times (6 sts).

Break the yarn and draw it tightly through the sts with a tapestry needle.

EYES

With Black, embroider eyes onto the front of the Body with 2 sts for each, placed about 3 sts back from the closed-up end and spaced about 4 sts apart.

EARS

With MC, embroider ears by wrapping yarn around one knitted st 4–5 times, placing the ears one st behind the eyes.

MANE

With CC and size 6 needles, CO 20 sts onto 3 needles and join in a round.
  Purl 1 round.
  BO all sts (knitwise).
  Fit the Mane around the Body, just behind the ears, and attach it using a back stitch.

LEGS (make 2)

With MC, CO 2 sts onto one needle.
  Work 11 rows of I-cord. Then break the yarn and draw it tightly through the sts.
  With the end still threaded on the tapestry needle, insert the I-cord from back to front on the underside of the Body. Pull the I-cord halfway through the Body, forming one front and one back leg. Weave the loose ends back up through the I-cord and the Body.

TAIL

With MC, pick up and knit 2 sts at the back of the Body, just above the small cast-on opening.
  Knit 4 rows of I-cord, then break the yarn and pull it tightly through the sts.
  Cut 2 strands of CC yarn and tie them to the end, then trim short.

FINISHING

Weave in loose ends.

Tiny Armadillo

He doesn't know what to do with himself since he isn't dead on the side of the road.

SPECIAL TECHNIQUES
Picking up stitches (page 20)
Kfbf = Knit into front of stitch, then knit into back of stitch, then into front again before slipping stitch off left needle (increases by 2 stitches)

YARN
Fingering-weight yarn in one color and black
Sample made with Koigu Premium Merino

(1/super fine; 100% wool; 1¾ oz/50g, 170 yd/155m)
Main Color: 2360
Black: 2400

OTHER SUPPLIES
Set of size 1 U.S. (2.25mm) double-pointed needles
Small tapestry needle
Stuffing

Tiny Armadillo is about 1¾" long, or 16 times tinier than a pickup truck tire.

BODY
CO 2 sts onto one needle.
   Knit 6 rows of I-cord.
Row 7 (work as I-cord): [Kfbf] twice (6 sts)
   Distribute sts onto 3 needles to work in a round.
Rnd 8: Knit.
Rnd 9: [Kfb] 6 times (12 sts).
Rnds 10–20: Knit (11 rnds).
   Stuff the piece.
Rnd 21: [K2tog] 6 times (6 sts).
   Break the yarn and draw it tightly through the sts using a tapestry needle. (Before attaching the Shell, the armadillo has a skinny shape.)

EYES
With Black, embroider eyes with 2 sts for each, placed about 3 sts from the closed-up end of the Body and spaced about 3 sts apart.

EARS (make 2)
Pick up and knit 2 sts just behind an eye.
   Knit 1 row of I-cord, then break the yarn and draw tightly through the sts with a tapestry needle.

LEGS (make 2)
CO 2 sts onto one needle.
   Knit 12 rows of I-cord, then break the yarn and draw it tightly through the sts with a tapestry needle.
   With the end still threaded on the tapestry needle, insert the I-cord from back to front on the underside of the Body. Pull the I-cord halfway through the Body, forming one front and one back leg. Weave the ends through the I-cord and the Body.

SHELL
CO 8 sts onto one needle to work straight.
Row 1: Knit.

Before attaching the Shell, the armadillo has a skinny shape.

Row 2: K2, [kfb] 4 times, k2 (12 sts).
Row 3: Knit.
Row 4: K1, [kfb, k2] 3 times, kfb, k1 (16 sts).
Rows 5–13: Knit.
Row 14: K1, [k2tog, k2] 3 times, k2tog, k1 (12 sts).
Row 15: Knit.
Row 16: K2, [k2tog] 4 times, k2 (8 sts).
   BO all sts.

FINISHING
Fit the Shell over the Body and sew in place with a few sts. Weave in the ends.

Tiny Edibles

Tiny Fried Eggs

Conjoined twins? Hardly. They're not even related!

SPECIAL TECHNIQUES
Mattress stitch (page 24)

YARN
Fingering-weight yarn in white, yellow, and black
Sample made with Koigu Premium Merino
(1/super fine; 100% wool; 1¾ oz/50g, 170 yd/155m)
White: 0000

Yellow: 1200
Black: 2400

OTHER SUPPLIES
Set of size 1 U.S. (2.25mm) double-pointed needles
Small tapestry needle
Stuffing

> Tiny Fried Eggs are about 2" long, or 3 times tinier than a pair of extra large fried eggs.

WHITES
With White, CO 3 sts onto one needle to work straight.
Row 1 and all odd-numbered rows through row 13: Purl.
Row 2: [Kfb] 3 times (6 sts).
Row 4: K1, kfb, k2, kfb, k1 (8 sts).
Row 6: K1, kfb, k4, kfb, k1 (10 sts).
Row 8: K1, [kfb] twice, k5, kfb, k1 (13 sts).
Rows 10 and 12: Knit.
Row 14: K1, k2tog, k5, [k2tog] twice, k1 (10 sts).
Row 15: P1, p2tog, p4, p2tog, p1 (8 sts).

Row 16: K1, kfb, k4, kfb, k1 (10 sts)
Odd-numbered rows 17–27: Purl.
Row 18: K1, kfb, k5, [kfb] twice, k1 (13 sts).
Rows 20 and 22: Knit.
Row 24: K1, [k2tog] twice, k5, k2tog, k1 (10 sts).
Row 26: K5, [k2tog] twice, k1 (8 sts).
Row 28: [K2tog] 4 times (4 sts).
BO all sts on the purl side.

YOLK *(make 2)*
With Yellow, CO 8 sts onto 3 needles and join in a round.
Rnd 1: [Kfb] 8 times (16 sts).
Rnds 2 and 3: Knit.
Rnd 4: [K2tog, k2] 4 times (12 sts).
Rnd 5: Knit.
Stuff the piece.
Rnd 6: [K2tog] 6 times (6 sts).
Break the yarn and draw it tightly through the sts with a tapestry needle.

FINISHING
Block the Whites by dampening the piece and laying it flat to dry.

Once the Whites are dry, center a Yolk on one half of the knit side of the Whites, with the closed-up end facing up. Attach the Yolk to the Whites using mattress stitch, stitching around the Yolk directly above its increase sts. Repeat to attach the second Yolk to the other half of the Whites.

With Black, embroider eyes on each Yolk with 2 small sts for each, placed about 3 sts apart.

Weave in loose ends.

Tiny Baked Potato

You can never have too much butter, unless the butter outweighs you by a significant margin.

YARN

Fingering-weight yarn in 4 colors and black
Sample made with Knit Picks Palette
(1/super fine; 100% wool; 1¾ oz/50g, 231 yd/211m)
Color 1 (skin): 24240 (Doe)
Color 2 (fluff): 23730 (Cream)
Color 3 (chives): 24585 (Grass)

Color 4 (butter): 24250 (Semolina)
Black: 23729

OTHER SUPPLIES

Set of size 1 U.S. (2.25mm) double-pointed needles
Small tapestry needle
Stuffing

> **Tiny Baked Potato is about 1" long, or 5 times tinier than the average russet potato.**

SKIN

With Color 1, CO 6 sts onto 3 needles and join in a round.

Rnd 1: [Kfb] 6 times (12 sts).

Rnd 2: Knit.

Rnd 3: [Kfb, k1] 6 times (18 sts).

Instead of continuing on to the first st in the next round, turn the piece to work straight.

Rows 4–11: Beginning with a purl row, work 8 rows in St st.

Once you finish the last knit row, rejoin to work in a round.

Rnd 12: Knit.

Rnd 13: [K2tog, k1] 6 times (12 sts)

Rnd 14: Knit.

Rnd 15: [K2tog] to end (6 sts).

Break the yarn and draw it tightly through the sts with a tapestry needle.

POTATO FLUFF

With Color 2, CO 10 sts onto one needle to work straight.

Work in garter stitch, knitting every row, for 14 rows.

BO all sts.

FINISHING

Stuff the Skin with stuffing, then insert the Fluff into the Skin so that the edges of the Fluff piece are tucked away, but the middle of the piece bulges out from the Skin. Stitch into place.

With Color 3, embroider chives onto the Fluff, making one small stitch for each.

With Color 4, embroider butter into the top of the Fluff, making 4-6 longer sts placed close together.

With Black yarn, embroider eyes using 2 small vertical sts for each, and spaced about 4 sts apart.

Weave in loose ends.

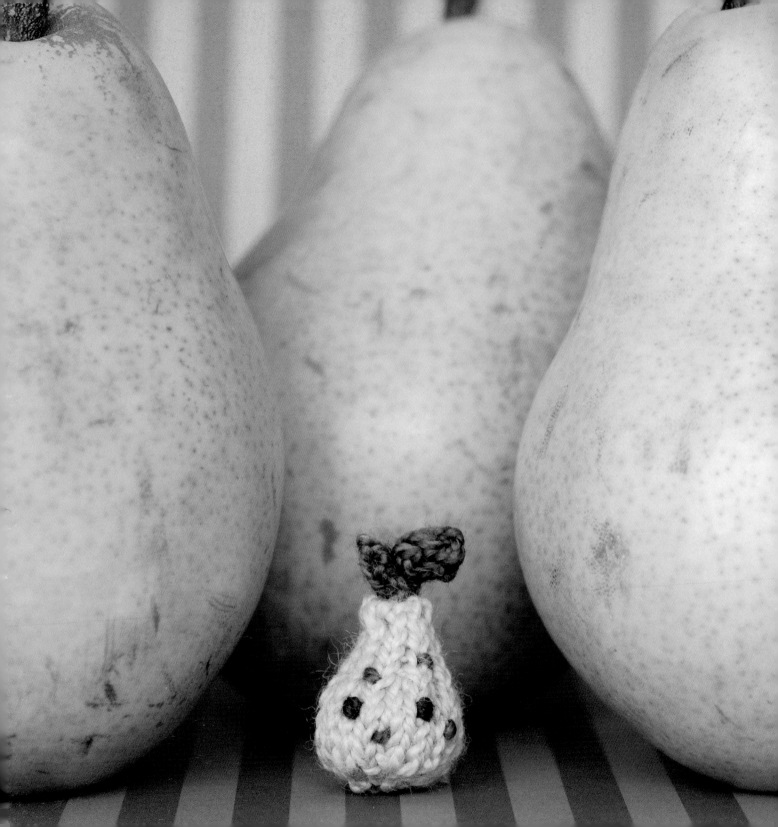

Tiny Pear

Her favorite Pear-Olympics event is pears skating.

SPECIAL TECHNIQUES
Picking up stitches (page 20)

YARN
Fingering-weight yarn in light green, brown, dark green, and black
Sample made with Koigu Premium Merino (1/super fine; 100% wool; 1¾ oz/50g, 170 yd/155m)

Light Green (body): 2132
Brown (stem and spots): 2395
Dark Green (leaf): 2330
Black: 2400

OTHER SUPPLIES
Set of size 1 U.S. (2.25mm) double-pointed needles
Small tapestry needle
Stuffing

Tiny Pear is about 1" tall, or 4 times tinier than a Green Anjou.

PEAR

With Light Green, CO 6 sts onto 3 needles and join in a round.

Rnd 1: [Kfb] 6 times (12 sts).

Rnd 2: [Kfb, k1] 6 times (18 sts).

Rnds 3–6: Knit (4 rnds).

Rnd 7: [K2tog] 9 times (9 sts)

Rnds 8–11: Knit (4 rnds).

Stuff the piece, then break the yarn and thread it loosely through the sts with a tapestry needle, leaving an open hole at the top.

STEM

With Brown, CO 3 sts onto one needle.

Work 5 rows of I-cord, then break the yarn and draw it tightly through the sts.

With the end still threaded on the tapestry needle, insert the I-cord down into the hole that you left at the top of the Pear, leaving most of the I-cord sticking out of the top.

Pull tightly on the loose yarn at the top of the Pear, then thread the end of the yarn onto a tapestry needle, and weave it back through the top and the Stem to secure the Stem into the Pear.

LEAF

With Dark Green, pick up and knit 2 sts on the side of the Stem to work straight.

Row 1 (work as I-cord): [Kfb] twice (4 sts).

Row 2 (work straight): Purl.

Row 3: Knit.

Break the yarn and draw it tightly through the sts with a tapestry needle, pulling the yarn across the purl side and inserting it into the opposite stitch.

FINISHING

With Black, embroider eyes onto the Pear using 2 small sts for each, spaced about 2 sts apart.

With Brown, embroider spots onto the Pear with one small st for each spot.

Weave in loose ends.

Tiny Corn

Genetically modified for cuteness!

> Tiny Corn is about 1" tall, or 8 times tinier than a real ear of corn.

CORN

With Yellow, CO 6 sts onto 3 needles and join in a round.
Rnd 1: Knit.
Rnd 2: [Kfb, k1] 3 times (9 sts).
Rnds 3–14: Knit (12 rnds).
Rnd 15: [K2tog, k1] 3 times (6 sts).

Break the yarn and draw it loosely through the sts with a tapestry needle.

Turn the piece inside out, stuff, then tighten up the sts at the top.

EYES

With Black, embroider eyes with 2 vertical sts per eye, spaced about 2 sts apart.

HUSK

Base

With Green, CO 6 sts onto 3 needles and join in a round.
First round: [Kfb] 6 times (12 sts).
Knit 2 more rounds.

Husks

Knit 4 sts, and turn to work these sts separately, leaving the remaining 8 sts on 2 other needles.

Beginning with a purl row, work 7 rows in St st.
Next row: [K2tog] twice (2 sts).

Break the yarn and draw it tightly through the sts with a tapestry needle.

Reattach the yarn to the next live stitch, and repeat the above section (after "Husks") twice more.

FINISHING

Tuck the Corn into the Husk, and secure it in place with a few sts that go straight through the Husk and the Corn.

Weave in loose ends.

Tiny Hot Dog

Just don't call him a cocktail weenie.

SPECIAL TECHNIQUES
Mattress stitch (page 24)
Back stitch (page 27)

YARN
Fingering-weight yarn in 3 colors and black
Sample made with Knit Picks Palette
(1/super fine; 100% wool; 1¾ oz/50g, 231 yd/211m)
Color 1 (bun): 24252 (Cornmeal)
Color 2 (dog): 24556 (Rose Hip)

Black: 23729
Koigu Premium Merino (1/super fine; 100% wool;
1¾ oz/50g, 170 yd/155m)
Color 3 (mustard): 2100

OTHER SUPPLIES
Set of size 1 U.S. (2.25mm) double-pointed needles
Small tapestry needle
Stuffing

> **Tiny Hot Dog is about 1" long, or 6 times tinier than a dog at Wrigley Field.**

BUN HALF (make 2)

With Color 1, CO 4 sts onto one needle.

Rnd 1 (work as I-cord): [Kfb] 4 times (8 sts).

Distribute the sts onto 3 needles to work in a round.

Knit 12 rounds.

Stuff the piece lightly, then break the yarn and draw it tightly through the sts with a tapestry needle.

DOG

With Color 2, CO 6 sts onto 3 needles and join in a round.

Knit 14 rounds.

Insert a small amount of stuffing.

Break the yarn and draw it tightly through the sts with a tapestry needle.

FINISHING

Align the Bun Halves parallel to each other, and beginning 2 sts from the ends, join together using mattress stitch (right). Stop sewing 2 sts from other ends of the Bun Halves.

Lay the Dog on the seam of the Bun Halves, and attach with a few sts.

With Black, embroider eyes using 2 small sts for each, spaced about 1½ sts apart.

With Color 3, embroider a curvy line of mustard onto the Dog using a back stitch.

Weave in loose ends.

Join the 2 Bun Halves together using mattress stitch.

Tiny Cupcakes

They may look sweet, but last week they got into a barroom brawl with a cinnamon roll.

SPECIAL TECHNIQUES
Mattress stitch (page 24)

YARN
Fingering-weight yarn in 3 colors and black
Samples made with Knit Picks Palette
(1/super fine; 100% wool; 1¾ oz/50g, 231 yd/211m)
Color 1 (cake): 24558 (Custard) or 24240 (Doe)
Color 2 (frosting): 24568 (Cosmopolitan), 23730

(Cream), or 23724 (Sky)
Color 3 (sprinkles): 23730 (Cream), 24568
(Cosmopolitan), or 24240 (Doe)
Black: 23729

OTHER SUPPLIES
Set of size 1 U.S. (2.25mm) double-pointed needles
Small tapestry needle
Stuffing

> Tiny Cupcakes are about 1" tall, or 3 times tinier than a gourmet New York City cupcake.

CAKE

With Color 1, CO 4 sts onto one needle.
Rnd 1 (work as I-cord): [Kfb] 4 times (8 sts).

Distribute sts onto 3 needles and join in a round.
Rnd 2: [Kfb] 8 times (16 sts).
Rnd 3: Knit.
Rnd 4: [Kfb, k1] 8 times (24 sts).
Rnd 5: [K1, p1] to end.
Rnds 6–9: Repeat rib pattern established in Rnd 5 (4 rnds).

Bind off all sts in the rib pattern.

FROSTING

With Color 2, CO 48 sts onto 3 needles and join in a round.
Rnd 1: [K2tog] 24 times (24 sts).
Rnds 2–5: Knit (4 rnds).
Rnd 6: [K2tog, k2] 6 times (18 sts).
Rnd 7: Knit.
Rnd 8: [K2tog] 9 times (9 sts).

Break the yarn and draw it tightly through the sts with a tapestry needle.

FINISHING

Turn the Cake piece inside out so the purl sts face out at the bottom. Place the Frosting on top of the Cake, with the outside edge of the Frosting overlapping the bound-off edge of the Cake. Use a mattress stitch to attach the underside of the Frosting edge to the edge of the Cake, attaching a few sts back from the edge of the Frosting (above, right).

Use mattress stitch to attach the underside of the Frosting piece to the Cake piece, attaching a few stitches back from the edge of the Frosting piece.

Stuff the piece before closing up the seam.

With Black, embroider eyes with 2 small sts for each, placed a few sts back from the edge of the Frosting and spaced about 4 sts apart.

With Color 3, embroider sprinkles onto the Frosting, making one longer stitch per sprinkle.

Weave in loose ends.

Tiny Humanoids

Tiny Babies

These guys are always crying when they want something. It's so immature!

YARN

Fingering-weight yarn in 5 colors and black
Samples made with Knit Picks Palette
(1/super fine; 100% wool; 1¾ oz/50g, 231 yd/211m)
Color 1 (diaper): 23730 (Cream)
Color 2 (skin): 24240 (Doe), 24252 (Cornmeal),
23718 (Blush)
Color 3 (diaper pin): 23724 (Sky)
Color 4 (mouth): 24553 (Serrano)

Color 5 (hair): 24562 (Bison), 23729 (Black), or
24240 (Doe)
Black: 23729

OTHER SUPPLIES

Set of size 1 U.S. (2.25mm) double-
pointed needles
Small tapestry needle
Stuffing

Tiny Babies are each about 1" tall, or about 27 times tinier than an average 6-month-old.

BODY (worked back to front)

With Color 1, CO 6 sts onto 3 needles and join in a round.

Rnd 1: [Kfb] 6 times (12 sts).
Rnd 2: [Kfb, k1] 6 times (18 sts).
Rnd 3: Knit.
Rnd 4: [Kfb, k2] 6 times (24 sts).
Rnds 5 and 6: Knit.
  Switch to Color 2.
Rnds 7–9: Knit.
Rnd 10: [K2tog, k2] 6 times (18 sts).
Rnds 11–14: Knit.
Rnd 15: [K2tog, k1] 6 times (12 sts).
  Stuff the piece.
Rnd 16: [K2tog] 6 times (6 sts).

Break the yarn and draw it tightly through the sts with a tapestry needle.

EYES

For a sitting baby, embroider eyes with Black onto the front of the Body with 2 sts for each, placed about 4 sts down from the top end and spaced about 3 sts apart.

For a crawling baby, embroider eyes onto front end of Body with 2 sts for each, placed about 2 sts back from the front end and spaced about 4 sts apart.

ARMS/LEGS (make 2)

With Color 2, CO 2 sts onto one needle. Knit 15 rounds of I-cord, then break the yarn and draw it tightly through the sts.

For a sitting baby, insert one I-cord through the sides of the Body, about 2 sts below the eyes, and pull halfway through the Body, leaving an even amount on each side. Weave the loose ends back through the I-cord and the head. Repeat with the second I-cord to make the legs, inserting it about 3 sts down from the color change on the Body.

For a crawling baby, turn the Body horizontally, and use each I-cord to make one leg and one arm on the underside of the Body (above, right).

For a crawling baby, turn the Body horizontally, and insert an I-cord from back to front to form one leg and one arm. Repeat for the second leg and arm.

FINISHING

With Color 3, embroider a diaper pin onto the sides of the diaper with one stitch across 1½ knitted sts.

Add a mouth with one stitch of Color 4, 2 sts down from the eyes (for a sitting baby) or just below the end of the Body (for a crawling baby).

For hair, thread a strand of Color 5 from the back of the Body (to secure) up through the front, above and between the eyes. Cut it short to form a tuft.

Weave in loose ends.

Tiny Mermaid

Like her mother said, there are plenty of fish in the sea. But she always ends up with a shrimp.

YARN

Fingering-weight yarn in 4 colors and black
Sample made with Koigu Premium Merino
(1/super fine; 100% wool; 1¾ oz/50g, 170 yd/155m)
Color 1 (skin): 1150.5
Color 2 (tail): 1520
Color 3 (bra): 1171
Color 4 (hair): 1265
Black: 2400

OTHER SUPPLIES

Set of size 1 U.S. (2.25mm) double-pointed needles
Small tapestry needle
Safety pin or spare knitting needle
Small crochet hook (size B U.S. [2.25mm])
Stuffing

> **Tiny Mermaid is about 2" tall, or 35 times tinier than Daryl Hannah in *Splash*.**

BODY

With Color 1, CO 6 sts onto 3 needles and join in a round.

Rnd 1: [Kfb] 6 times (12 sts).

Rnd 2: Knit.

Rnd 3: [M1, k2] 6 times (18 sts).

Rnds 4–9: Knit (6 rnds).

Switch to Color 2.

Rnds 10–12: Knit.

Rnd 13: [K2tog, k4] 3 times (15 sts).

Rnd 14: Knit.

Rnd 15: [K2tog, k3] 3 times (12 sts).

Rnd 16: Knit.

Rnd 17: [K2tog, k2] 3 times (9 sts).

Rnd 18: Knit.

Stuff the piece.

Rnd 19: [K2tog, k1] 3 times (6 sts)

Separate fins

Place the first 3 sts in the round onto one needle, and place the last 3 onto a safety pin or spare needle to work later.

Next round (work as I-cord): [Kfb] 3 times (6 sts).

Distribute the sts onto 3 needles, and knit 2 rounds.

Break the yarn, leaving a long tail of about 12", and draw it tightly through the sts with a tapestry needle.

Place the held sts onto one needle. With the loose end still threaded on the tapestry needle, weave the loose end back through the fin and attach it to the last live stitch ( above, right).

Work the second fin the same as the first.

Ⓐ After finishing the first fin, weave the loose end back through the fin, and attach it to the last live stitch in the separate group of stitches.

EYES

With Black, embroider eyes with 2 sts for each, placed about 5 sts from the top of the head and spaced about 3 sts apart.

ARMS

With Color 1, CO 2 sts onto one needle.

Knit 16 rows of I-cord, then break the yarn and draw it tightly through the sts with a tapestry needle.

With the end still threaded on the tapestry needle, insert the I-cord through the Body, going in and coming out at about 2 sts below and 2 sts outside the eyes. Pull the I-cord halfway through, leaving an even amount on each side. Weave the loose ends back through the I-cord and the Body.

BRA

With Color 3, embroider bra shells with 3 vertical sts for each. Begin each st at its lower side (one st above the color change on the Body, and directly below the eye), radiating outward from a single point at the bottom (B, right, above). For the bra strap, cut a strand of Color 3, and thread it horizontally under both shells' stitches (C, right). Tie in a bow at the back of the Body. Then, with another strand of Color 3, stitch the bow in place so it won't come untied (D. above, far right).

B Embroider the bra shells with 3 vertical stitches for each, with the stitches beginning just above the Mermaid's tail.

C For the bra strap, thread a strand of yarn under both shell stitches

D Tie the bra strap in a bow at the back of the Mermaid's Body, then stitch it in place to secure.

HAIR

For hair, cut 8–10 approximately 5"-long strands of Color 4. Fold each strand in half and weave it under a stitch on the Mermaid's head using the crochet hook. Slip the ends of the yarn through the resulting loop and pull to tighten.

Once you have attached all the hair, trim the ends to the desired length.

FINISHING

Weave in loose ends.

Tiny Gnome

He just returned from a trip to Nome, Alaska, where he was very disappointed not to find a G.

SPECIAL TECHNIQUES

Back stitch (page 27)

YARN

Fingering-weight yarn in 5 colors and black
Sample made with Koigu Premium Merino
(1/super fine; 100% wool; 1³⁄₄ oz/50g, 170 yd/155m)
Color 1 (pants): 2395
Color 2 (shirt): 2310
Color 3 (face): 1150.5

Color 4 (hat): 2220
Color 5 (beard): 0000
Black: 2400

OTHER SUPPLIES

Set of size 1 U.S. (2.25mm) double-pointed needles
Small tapestry needle
Small crochet hook
(size B U.S. [2.25mm] recommended)
Stuffing

Tiny Gnome is about 1¹⁄₄" tall, or 9¹⁄₂ times tinier than the average garden gnome.

BODY

With Color 1, CO 4 sts onto one needle.

Knit 2 rows of I-cord, then break the yarn and set aside on a spare needle.

Make a second leg the same way as the first, without breaking the yarn.

Join legs

Divide the sts of each leg onto 2 needles, with the working yarn attached to the rightmost stitch on the back needle.

Knit one round, starting with the needle in front, then flipping needles around and continuing on with the back needle.

Distribute 8 sts onto 3 needles to continue to work in a round.

Shape Body

Rnd 1: [Kfb] 8 times (16 sts).

Rnd 2: [Kfb, k1] 8 times (24 sts).

Switch to Color 2.

Rnds 3–7: Knit (5 rnds).

Switch to Color 3.

Rnd 8: [K2tog, k1] 8 times (16 sts).

Rnds 9–11: Knit.

Switch to Color 4.

Rnds 12–14: Knit.

Rnd 15: [K2tog, k2] 4 times (12 sts).

Rnds 16 and 17: Knit.

Stuff the piece.

Rnd 18: [K2tog, k1] 4 times (8 sts).

Rnd 19: Knit.

Rnd 20: [K2tog] 4 times (4 sts).

Break the yarn and draw it tightly through the sts with a tapestry needle.

EYES

With Black, embroider eyes with 2 sts for each, midway down the face and spaced about 2 sts apart.

ARMS

With Color 2, CO 2 sts onto one needle.

Knit 16 rows of I-cord, then break the yarn and draw it tightly through the sts with a tapestry needle.

With the end still threaded on the tapestry needle, insert the I-cord through the Body, going in and coming out at the sides of the Body, just below the color change. Weave the loose ends back up through the I-cord and the Body.

BEARD

With Color 5, CO 8 sts onto one needle to work straight, leaving a tail for attaching.

Row 1: Knit.

Row 2: K2tog, k to last 2 sts, k2tog.

Repeat these 2 rows until there are 2 sts on your needle.

Break the yarn and draw it tightly through the sts with a tapestry needle.

FINISHING

Attach the cast-on edge of the beard to the bottom row of Color 3 sts using a back stitch.

Weave in loose ends.

Tiny Alien

Take him to your lederhosen! (He's a big Germanophile.)

YARN

Fingering-weight yarn in 2 colors and black
Sample made with Koigu Premium Merino
(1/super fine; 100% wool; 1¾ oz/50g, 170 yd/155m)
Main Color (MC) (body): 1520
Contrasting Color (CC) (antennae): 2100
Black: 2400

OTHER SUPPLIES

Set of size 1 U.S. (2.25mm) double-pointed needles
Small tapestry needle
Stuffing

> Tiny Alien is about 1" tall, or 42 times tinier than E. T.

BODY

With MC, CO 3 sts onto one needle. Knit 2 rows of I-cord, then break the yarn and set aside on a spare needle.

Make a second leg the same way as the first, without breaking the yarn.

Join legs

Place the held sts of the first leg onto the same needle as the second leg, with the working yarn on the left. Bring the yarn around in the back to the first st, and knit across both legs (6 sts).

Distribute the sts onto 3 needles to continue to work in a round.

Shape body

Rnd 1: [Kfb] 6 times (12 sts).
Rnd 2: Knit.
Rnd 3: K2, [kfb] twice, k4, [kfb] twice, k2 (16 sts).
Rnd 4: Knit.
Rnd 5: K3, [kfb] twice, k6, [kfb] twice, k3 (20 sts).
Rnds 6–10: Knit (5 rnds).
Rnd 11: [K2tog] 10 times (10 sts).
Rnd 12: Knit.

Stuff the piece, then break the yarn and draw it tightly through the sts with a tapestry needle.

EYES

With Black, embroider eyes with 4 sts for each across 1½ knitted sts, placed about 6 sts from the top of the Body and spaced 2 sts apart.

ARMS

With MC, CO 2 sts onto one needle. Knit 10 rows of I-cord, then break the yarn and draw it tightly through the sts with a tapestry needle.

With the end still threaded on the tapestry needle, insert the I-cord through the sides of the Body, just above the legs. Pull the I-cord halfway through the Body, leaving an even amount on each side. Weave the loose ends back through the arms and the Body.

ANTENNAE

With CC, CO 2 sts and work 10 rows of I-cord.

With the end still threaded on the tapestry needle, insert the I-cord through the top of the head. Pull the I-cord halfway through the head so antennae are equal in height. Weave the loose ends back through the antennae and the Body.

FINISHING

Weave in loose ends.

Tiny Bride and Groom

According to their prenuptial agreement, if they split up, she takes the cake.

SPECIAL TECHNIQUES
Back stitch (page 27)
Stranded color knitting (page 139)

YARN
Fingering-weight yarn in 5 colors, including black
Samples made with Koigu Premium Merino
(1/super fine; 100% wool; 1¾ oz/50g, 170 yd/155m)
Color 1 (dress): 0000

Color 2 (skin): 1150.5
Color 3 (Bride's hair): 2100
Color 4 (tuxedo and eyes): 2400
Color 5 (Groom's hair): 2395

OTHER SUPPLIES
Set of size 1 U.S. (2.25mm) double-pointed needles
Small tapestry needle
Stuffing

Tiny Bride and Groom are each about 1" tall, or 12 times tinier than a 3-tiered wedding cake.

Note: The Bride can stand alone, but the Groom will need a little help.

BRIDE

With Color 1, CO 24 sts onto 3 needles and join in a round.

Rnd 1: Knit.
Rnd 2: Purl.
Rnd 3: Knit.
Rnd 4: [K2tog, k2] 6 times (18 sts).
Rnd 5: Purl.
Rnd 6: Knit.
Rnd 7: [K2tog, k1] 6 times (12 sts).
Rnd 8: Purl.
Rnd 9: Knit.

Switch to Color 2.
Rnd 10: [K2tog] 6 times (6 sts).
Rnd 11: [Kfb] 6 times (12 sts).
Rnd 12: [Kfb, k2] 4 times (16 sts).
Rnds 13–16: Knit.
Rnd 17: [K2tog, k2] 4 times (12 sts).

Insert a small amount of stuffing inside the head section. (The dress will remain unstuffed.)

Rnd 18: [K2tog] 6 times (6 sts).

Break the yarn and draw it tightly through the sts with a tapestry needle.

EYES

With Black, embroider eyes with 2 sts for each, placed halfway down the head and spaced about 3 sts apart.

ARMS

With Color 2, CO 2 sts onto one needle.

Knit 10 rows of I-cord, then break the yarn and draw it tightly through the sts with a tapestry needle.

With the end still threaded on the tapestry needle, insert the I-cord through the body, under the top ruffle on the dress and just outside the eyes. Pull the I-cord halfway through, leaving an even amount on each side. Weave in the ends.

VEIL

With Color 1, CO 6 sts onto one needle to work straight.

Row 1: Knit.
Row 2: K1, kfb, k to last 2 sts, kfb, k1 (8 sts).
Row 3 and all odd-numbered rows: Purl.
Row 4: Knit.
Row 6: Work same as Row 2 (10 sts).
Row 8: Knit.
Row 10: Work same as Row 2 (12 sts).
Row 12: Knit.

Finish with a purl row, then BO all sts.

FINISHING BRIDE

Block the Veil by dampening it and laying it flat to dry.

With Color 3, embroider hair on the Bride's head by making long, loose sts that begin at the gathered sts at the top of the head and end at the top purl ridge on the dress (Ⓐ, below).

Ⓐ Embroider hair on the Bride's head with long, loose stitches that begin at the top of her head and end at the top of her dress.

Attach the cast-on edge of the Veil to the top of the head with a few sts.

Weave in loose ends.

GROOM

With Color 4, CO 3 sts onto one needle.

Knit 2 rows of I-cord, then break the yarn and set it aside on a spare needle.

Make a second leg the same way as the first, without breaking yarn.

Join legs

Place the held sts of the first leg on the same needle as the second leg, with the working yarn attached to the leftmost st. Bring the yarn around in the back to the first st, and knit across both legs (6 sts).

Distribute the sts onto 3 needles to continue to work in a round.

Shape body

Rnd 1: [Kfb] 6 times (12 sts).

Rnd 2: [Kfb, k2] 4 times (16 sts).

Beginning with Round 3, you will integrate Color 1 into the knitting.

Rnd 3: K6 Color 4, k4 Color 1, k6 Color 4.

Notes: When working with 2 colors, be sure to maintain an even tension, without pulling the first stitch too tightly.

Twist the strands of yarn together when switching colors to prevent gaps.

Rnds 4 and 5: Work same as Round 3. Switch to Color 2.

Rnd 6: [K2tog] 8 times (8 sts).

Rnd 7: [Kfb] 8 times (16 sts).

Rnds 8–11: Knit.

Rnd 12: [K2tog, k2] 4 times (12 sts).

Stuff the piece.

Rnd 13: [K2tog] 6 times (6 sts).

Break the yarn and draw it tightly through sts with a tapestry needle.

EYES

With Black, embroider eyes with 2 sts for each, placed halfway down the head and spaced about 3 sts apart.

ARMS

With Color 4, CO 2 sts onto one needle.

Knit 10 rows of I-cord, then break the yarn and draw it tightly through the sts with a tapestry needle.

With the end still threaded on the tapestry needle, insert the I-cord through the body, just to the outside of the Color 1 section. Pull the I-cord halfway through, leaving an even amount on each side. Weave in the ends.

Ⓑ Embroider hair on the Groom's head with short, tight stitches that begin at the top of his head and go down a few stitches from the top.

FINISHING GROOM

With Color 5, embroider hair on the Groom's head by making small, tight sts that go from the gathered sts at the top of the head to a few sts down the head (Ⓑ, above). For sideburns, make a vertical row of small horizontal sts at the sides of the head.

With Black, embroider the bow tie in 2 halves onto the top of the Color 1 section, with 3 small horizontal sts for each half.

Weave in loose ends.

Tiny Caveman

He's pretty psyched about discovering fire! Next he wants to discover his inner child.

SPECIAL TECHNIQUES
Picking up stitches (page 20)

YARN
Fingering-weight yarn in 3 colors and black
Sample made with Koigu Premium Merino
(1/super fine; 100% wool; 1¾ oz/50g, 170 yd/155m)
Color 1 (body): 1205
Color 2 (animal skin): 1265
Color 3 (spots, hair, and club): 2395
Black: 2400

OTHER SUPPLIES
Set of size 1 U.S. (2.25mm) double-pointed needles
Small tapestry needle
Small crochet hook (size B U.S. [2.25mm])
Stuffing

BODY

With Color 1, CO 4 sts onto one needle.

Knit 2 rows of I-cord, then break the yarn and set aside on a spare needle.

Make a second leg the same way as the first, without breaking the yarn.

Join legs

Divide the sts of each leg onto 2 needles, with the first 2 sts of each leg adjacent to each other on one needle, and the last 2 sts of each leg adjacent to each other on the other needle. Hold the needles parallel to each other, with the working yarn attached to the rightmost st on the back needle.

Knit one round, starting with the needle in front, then flipping the needles around and continuing on with the back needle.

Distribute 8 sts onto 3 needles to continue to work in a round.

Shape body

Rnd 1: [Kfb] 8 times (16 sts).
Rnd 2: [Kfb, k1] 8 times (24 sts).
Rnds 3–11: Knit (9 rounds).
Rnd 12: [K2tog, k2] 6 times (18 sts).
Rnd 13: Knit.
Rnd 14: [K2tog, k1] 6 times (12 sts).
Stuff the piece.
Rnd 15: [K2tog] 6 times (6 sts).

Break the yarn and draw it tightly through the sts with a tapestry needle.

Sew up the gap between the legs with a couple of small sts.

EYES

With Black, embroider the eyes with 2 sts for each, placed about 5 sts from the top of the head and spaced about 3 sts apart.

ARMS

With Color 1, CO 2 sts onto one needle.

Knit 22 rows of I-cord, then break the yarn and draw it tightly through the sts with a tapestry needle.

With the end still threaded on the tapestry needle, insert the I-cord through the Body, going in and coming out at the sides of the Body and about 3 sts below the eyes. Pull the I-cord halfway through, leaving an even amount on each side. Weave the loose ends back through the I-cord and the Body.

ANIMAL SKIN

With Color 2, CO 24 sts onto 3 needles and join in a round.

Knit 10 rounds.

Cut the yarn, leaving a long tail of approximately 14".

Thread the tail onto a tapestry needle, and slip the needle under the second and first sts in the round, from left to right (A below.)

A To form the bottom edge of the Animal Skin, cut a long tail of yarn, thread it onto a tapestry needle, and slip the needle under the second and first sts in the round, from left to right.

Pull tightly through the sts without slipping the sts off the needle. Slip the tapestry needle through the same way twice more, then slip 2 sts off the needle.

Weave the tail end down through the purl side of the piece and back up to attach to the next live st (**B**, below).

B After slipping 2 stitches off the left needle, weave the tail back through the purl side of the piece, and attach it to the next live stitch.

Repeat with every 2 sts in the round until the bottom edge is finished.

Form strap

Turn the piece over, and pick up and knit 3 sts at the top edge (**C** below.)

C To begin making the strap on the Animal Skin, pick up and knit 3 stitches at the top of the skin piece.

Turn, and beginning with a purl row, work 9 rows St st.

BO sts, leaving a tail for attaching.

Fit the Animal Skin over the Body, with the strap in front of the right arm.

Fold the strap over arm, and attach it to the cast-on edge of the Animal Skin using mattress stitch where the strap and the Animal Skin meet up (**D** below.)

D Once you have made the strap, fit the Animal Skin over the Body, fold the strap over the arm, and attach the strap to the cast-on edge of the skin using mattress stitch.

CLUB

With Color 3, CO 3 sts onto one needle.

Knit 6 rows of I-cord.

Row 7 (work as I-cord): [Kfb] 3 times (6 sts).

Distribute the sts onto 3 needles to continue to work in a round.

Round 8: Knit.

Round 9: [Kfb, k1] 3 times (9 sts).

Rounds 10–12: Knit.

Insert a small amount of stuffing into the piece.

Break the yarn and draw it tightly through the sts with a tapestry needle.

FINISHING

With Color 3, embroider spots onto the Animal Skin, with one small stitch per spot. You can go straight through the Body, attaching the Animal Skin to the Body as you embroider.

For hair, cut 4–6 approximately 5"-long strands of Color 3. Fold each strand in half and weave it under a stitch on the Caveman's head using the crochet hook. Slip the yarn ends through the loop and pull to tighten.

Trim the yarn ends to the desired length. Then, using one blade of a pair of scissors, split each strand of hair to give it a messy look.

Attach the I-cord end of the Club to the hand with a few stitches.

Weave in loose ends.

Tiny Caveman is about 1½" tall, or 54 times tinier than the average Cro-Magnon man.

Tiny Robots

Each one is quite sure that the other has a few screws loose.

SPECIAL TECHNIQUES
Picking up stitches (page 20)
Back stitch (page 27)

YARN
Fingering-weight yarn in 3 colors and black
Samples made with Knit Picks Palette
(1/super fine; 100% wool; 1¾ oz/50g, 231 yd/211m)
Color 1 (body): 24250 (Semolina) or 24583 (Cyan)
Color 2 (head, arms, and legs): 23733 (Mist)

Color 3 (buttons): 24583 (Cyan) or 24250
(Semolina)
Black: 23729

OTHER SUPPLIES
Set of size 1 U.S. (2.25mm) double-
pointed needles
Small tapestry needle
Stuffing

Tiny Robots are about 1" tall, or 51 times tinier than ASIMO.

BODY (worked bottom to top)
With Color 1, CO 6 sts onto 3 needles and join in a round.
Rnd 1: [Kfb] 6 times (12 sts).
Rnd 2: Knit.
Rnd 3: [Kfb, k1] 6 times (18 sts).
Rnds 4 and 5: Knit.
Rnd 6: [Kfb, k2] 6 times (24 sts).
Rnds 7–9: Knit.
Rnd 10: [K2tog, k2] 6 times (18 sts).
Rnds 11 and 12: Knit.
Rnd 13: [K2tog, k1] 6 times (12 sts).
  Stuff the piece, then break the yarn and draw it tightly through the sts with a tapestry needle.

HEAD
With Color 2, CO 14 sts onto 3 needles and join in a round.
  Knit 7 rounds.
Rnd 8: [K2tog] 7 times (7 sts).
  Break the yarn and draw it tightly through the sts with a tapestry needle.

Stuff the Head, and place it on top of the Body. Sew the cast-on edge of the Head to the Body using back stitch.

EYES
With Black, embroider eyes with 2 sts for each, placed midway down the Head and spaced about 3 sts apart.

ARMS (make 2)
With Color 2, pick up and knit 2 sts at the side of the Body, about 2 sts below the Head.
  Knit 6 rows of I-cord.
Next row (work as I-cord): [Kfb] twice (4 sts).
  Knit one more row of I-cord.
  Break the yarn and draw it tightly through the sts with a tapestry needle.

LEGS (make 2)
With Color 2, pick up and knit 2 sts at the second increase round on the Body, spaced 4 sts apart.

Knit 1 row of I-cord.
Next row (work as I-cord): [Kfb] twice (4 sts).
  Knit one more row of I-cord.
  Break the yarn and draw it tightly through the sts with a tapestry needle.

ANTENNA
With Color 2, CO 2 sts onto one needle.
  Knit 4 rows of I-cord, then break the yarn and draw it tightly through the sts with a tapestry needle.
  With the end still threaded on the tapestry needle, thread the I-cord down through the top of the Head, and stitch in place.

FINISHING
With Color 3, embroider buttons onto the Body with 2 sts per button, spaced as shown.
Weave in loose ends.

Tiny Inanimates

Tiny Airplane

Her guilty pleasure is to simulate turbulence just for fun.

> **Tiny Airplane is about 2" long with a 2½" wingspan, or 1,392 times tinier than a Boeing 747.**

FUSELAGE *(worked back to front)*

With MC, CO 6 sts onto 3 needles and join in a round.

Rnd 1: [Kfb] 6 times (12 sts).

Knit 22 rounds.

Stuff the piece.

Next round: [K2tog] 6 times (6 sts).

Break the yarn and draw it tightly through the sts with a tapestry needle.

EYES

With Black, embroider eyes with 2 sts for each, placed 3 sts from the front and spaced about 3 sts apart.

WINGS *(make 2)*

With MC, pick up and knit horizontal 6 sts on the Fuselage, beginning 5 sts back from an eye (, above, right). Flip the piece, and pick up and knit 6 more sts with a second needle, parallel to first 6 (, right).

Join, and knit one round.

Distribute the sts onto 3 needles, and knit 10 more rounds.

A To make a Wing, start by picking up and knitting 6 stitches on the Fuselage, beginning 5 stitches back from one eye.

B After picking up the first 6 stitches for a Wing, turn the piece over, and pick up and knit 6 more stitches parallel to the first 6. Join these 12 stitches together to knit in a round.

Rnd 12: [K2tog, k1] 4 times (8 sts).

Rnd 13: Knit.

Without stuffing the piece, break the yarn and draw it tightly through the sts.

TAIL

With MC, pick up and knit 4 sts at the top of the back end of the Fuselage. Flip the piece around, and pick up and knit 4 more sts with a second needle, parallel to the first 4 sts.

Join, and knit 2 rounds.

Next round: K2, [k2tog] twice, k2 (6 sts).

Break the yarn and draw it tightly through the sts.

FINISHING

With CC and a tapestry needle, embroider a line of windows on each side of the plane, with one stitch per window, just above each wing. Go back over these stitches a second time. Weave in the ends.

Tiny Computer

These two haven't spoken to each other since 1998, when the mouse mentioned something about a system upgrade.

SPECIAL TECHNIQUES
Stranded color knitting (page 139)
Picking up stitches (page 20)

YARN
Fingering-weight yarn in 2 colors and black
Sample made with Knit Picks Palette
(1/super fine; 100% wool; 1¾ oz/50g, 231 yd/211m)
Main Color (MC) (computer): 23733 (Mist)
Contrasting Color (CC) (screen): 24583 (Cyan)
Black: 23729

OTHER SUPPLIES
Set of size 1 U.S. (2.25 mm) double-pointed needles
Stitch marker
Small tapestry needle
Stuffing

Tiny Computer is about 1¼" tall, or 4 times tinier than a floppy disk.

Note: When working with multiple colors, twist the strands of yarn together every few stitches to keep an even tension.

MONITOR

With MC, CO 12 sts onto one needle to work straight.

Row 1: Purl.

For Rows 2–7, incorporate CC as indicated, and twist MC around CC every few sts in CC section to keep an even tension.

Row 2: K2 MC, k8 CC, k2 MC.

Row 3: P2 MC, p8 CC, p2 MC.

Rows 4–7: Work as established, repeating Rows 2 and 3 twice more.

Drop CC, and continue with MC only.

Rows 8–10: Work 3 rows in St st, finishing with a knit row.

Instead of turning for the next purl row, rotate the piece 90 degrees clockwise, and pick up and knit 7 sts along the side of the piece with a second needle (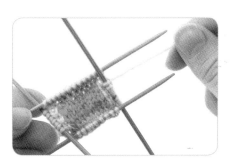, below). With a third needle, pick up and knit 10 sts from the cast-on edge. With a fourth needle, pick up and knit 7 sts along the remaining side.

Ⓐ After finishing the screen, turn the piece, and pick up and knit stitches around the other 3 sides of the piece. You will then distribute the stitches onto 3 needles before continuing to knit in a round to shape the monitor.

Distribute the sts onto 3 needles, and place a marker. You will continue to knit these 36 sts in the round.

Rnds 1–3: Knit.

Rnd 4: [K2tog, k4] 6 times (30 sts).

Rnds 5, 7, and 9: Knit.

Rnd 6: [K2tog, k3] 6 times (24 sts).

Rnd 8: [K2tog, k2] 6 times (18 sts).

Stuff the piece.

Rnd 10: [K2tog, k1] 6 times (12 sts)

Rnd 11: [K2tog] 6 times (6 sts)

Break the yarn and draw it through the sts with a tapestry needle.

KEYBOARD

(worked back to front)

With MC, CO 20 sts onto 3 needles, leaving a tail for seaming, and join in a round.

Knit 10 rounds.

Divide sts onto 2 needles, with 10 sts on each needle, and BO using kitchener stitch.

Without stuffing the piece, sew up the open end using mattress stitch.

MOUSE

Cord

With MC, CO 2 sts onto one needle.

Work as I-cord until 1¼" long, or for 16 rows.

Mouse

Row 1 (work as I-cord): [Kfb] twice (4 sts).

Row 2 (work as I-cord): [Kfb] 4 times (8 sts).

Distribute sts onto 3 needles and continue to work in a round.

Rnd 3: Knit.

Rnd 4: K2, [kfb] 4 times, k2 (12 sts).

Rnds 5–7: Knit.

Rnd 8: K2, [k2tog] 4 times, k2 (8 sts).

Insert a small amount of stuffing into the piece, then break the yarn and draw it tightly through sts with a tapestry needle.

FINISHING

With Black, embroider eyes onto the Monitor using 2 sts for each, spaced 3 sts apart. Embroider eyes onto the Mouse with one small st for each, spaced 3 sts apart.

Embroider 2 rows of keys onto the Keyboard, with 3 sts for the back row and 4 sts for the front row.

Attach the Monitor to the Keyboard using mattress stitch, with the sts landing on the second row of sts on the Keyboard (**B**, below).

Attach the Mouse to the back of the Keyboard with a few sts. Weave in the ends.

B Attach the Monitor to the Keyboard using mattress stitch.

Tiny Mailbox

He gets so many letters, and never is one addressed to him. (But he's kind of a jerk, so you don't have to feel sorry for him.)

SPECIAL TECHNIQUES
Picking up stitches (page 20)

YARN
Fingering-weight yarn in 5 colors and black
Sample made with Koigu Premium Merino
(1/super fine; 100% wool; 1³⁄₄ oz/50g, 170 yd/155m)
Color 1 (grass): 1520
Color 2 (pole): 2395
Color 3 (box): 2392
Color 4 (flag): 2220
Color 5 (letter): 0000
Black: 2400

OTHER SUPPLIES
Set of size 1 U.S. (2.25mm) double-pointed needles
Small tapestry needle
Stuffing

Tiny Mailbox is about 2¹⁄₄" tall, or 24 times tinier than a residential mailbox.

GRASS

With Color 1, CO 15 sts onto one needle to work straight.
Row 1: [K1, p1] to last st, k1.
Rows 2–22: Work same as Row 1.
BO all sts as established.

POLE

With Color 2, CO 12 sts onto 3 needles and join in a round.
Knit 12 rounds, then BO all sts.

BOX

With Color 3, CO 3 sts onto one needle to work straight.
Row 1: [Kfb] 3 times (6 sts).
Row 2: Purl.
Row 3: K1, kfb, k2, kfb, k1 (8 sts).
Row 4–9: Work 6 rows St st, finishing with a knit row.

Instead of turning for the next purl row, rotate the piece clockwise and pick up and knit 13 evenly spaced sts around the perimeter of piece using 2 additional needles (Ⓐ, below).

Ⓐ After finishing the flat back of the mailbox, turn the piece and pick up and knit 13 stitches around the sides of the piece. You will continue to knit in a round to form the sides of the box.

Continue to work these 21 sts in a round.

Knit 10 rounds.

Next round: K8, BO to end, binding off last st using the first st of the previous round. You will be left with one st on your right needle and 7 sts on your left.

Continue to knit to the end of the row, then turn the piece to work straight.

Shape flap

Rows 1–3: Beginning with a purl row, work 3 rows in St st.

Row 4: K1, k2tog, k2, k2tog, k1 (6 sts).

Row 5: Purl.

Row 6: K1, [k2tog] twice, k1 (4 sts).

BO all sts on the wrong side.

FLAG

With Color 4, CO 3 sts onto one needle, and work 8 rows of I-cord.

Break the yarn, leaving a long tail of about 11", and thread it through the sts, pulling tightly. Turn the piece 90 degrees clockwise, and with the yarn tail still attached, pick up and knit 4 sts down the side of the I-cord ( , above, right).

After knitting the I-cord for the flag, turn the piece sideways, and pick up and knit 4 stitches to knit the sideways section.

Turn, and beginning with a knit row, work 4 rows in St st.

BO all sts.

LETTER

With Color 5, CO 8 sts onto one needle to work straight.

Beginning with a purl row, work 7 rows in St st.

Row 8: K1, k2tog, k2, k2tog, k1 (6 sts).

Row 9: Purl.

Row 10: K1, [k2tog] twice, k1 (4 sts).

Row 11: [P2tog] twice (2 sts).

Break the yarn and draw it through the sts with a tapestry needle.

With the tail end still threaded through the tapestry needle, fold the pointed flap over and tack it down with a few sts.

FINISHING

With Black, embroider eyes onto the Box using 2 sts for each, spaced about 2 sts apart.

Place the Flag against the left side of the Box so that the knit side faces out, and attach with a few sts.

Attach one open end of the Pole to the underside of the Box using a mattress stitch. Stuff the Pole, and attach the remaining open end to the center of the Grass.

With Black, embroider eyes onto the Letter using one small stitch for each. If desired, tack the letter to the inside of the Box.

Weave in loose ends.

Tiny Sailboats

They plan to sail to the Far East someday—by which they mean the puddle down the street.

SPECIAL TECHNIQUES
Kitchener stitch (page 140)
Back stitch (page 27)

YARN
Fingering-weight yarn in 5 colors and black
Samples made with Koigu Premium Merino
(1/super fine; 100% wool; 1¾ oz/50g, 170 yd/155m)
Color 1 (boat): 1265, 1200, 2100

Color 2 (sail): 0000
Color 3 (pole): 2392
Black: 2400

OTHER SUPPLIES
Set of size 1 U.S. (2.25mm) double-pointed needles
Small tapestry needle
Stuffing

Each Tiny Sailboat is about 1½" tall, or 280 times tinier than a Catalina Sloop.

BOAT

With Color 1, CO 24 sts onto 3 needles, leaving a tail for seaming, and join in a round.
Rnds 1 and 2: Knit.
Rnd 3: K2tog, k8, [k2tog] twice, k8, k2tog (20 sts).
Rnd 4: Knit.
Rnd 5: K2tog, k6, [k2tog] twice, k6, k2tog (16 sts).
Rnd 6: Knit.
Rnd 7: K2tog, k4, [k2tog] twice, k4, k2tog (12 sts).
   Divide sts evenly onto 2 needles, and BO using kitchener stitch.

SAIL

With Color 2, CO 10 sts onto one needle to work straight.
Row 1: Purl.
Row 2: K1, k2tog, k to end (9 sts).
Row 3: Purl.

Repeat Rows 2 and 3 until there are 5 sts on your needles.
Next RS row: K1, [k2tog] twice (3 sts).
   Break the yarn and draw it tightly through the sts with a tapestry needle.

POLE

With Color 3, CO 3 sts onto one needle.
   Knit 14 rows of I-cord, then break the yarn and draw it tightly through the sts with a tapestry needle.

FINISHING

Place the left edge of the Sail against the Pole. Attach the top and the bottom edges of the Sail to the Pole with a few sts.
   Lightly stuff the Boat, and place the Pole inside the Boat, just to the left of the center, so that the bottom edge of the Sail touches the top edge of the Boat (above, right).

When sewing up the top of the Boat, place the Pole inside and sew it in place.

Begin sewing the cast-on edge of the Boat closed using a back stitch, and sew the Pole in place with a back stitch when you get to it.
   Attach the bottom right corner of the Sail to the top of the Boat.
   With Black, embroider eyes on the Boat using 2 small sts for each, spaced about 3 sts apart. Weave in the ends.

Tiny Record Player

Friends say he's a nice guy, even if he tends to repeat himself.

SPECIAL TECHNIQUES
Kitchener stitch (page 140)
Mattress stitch (page 24)

YARN
Fingering-weight yarn in 3 colors and black
Sample made with Koigu Premium Merino
(1/super fine; 100% wool; 1¾ oz/50g, 170 yd/155m)
Color 1 (record label): 2100

Color 2 (base): 2130
Color 3 (arm and buttons): 2392
Black: 2400

OTHER SUPPLIES
Set of size 1 U.S. (2.25mm) double-pointed needles
Small tapestry needle
Stuffing

> **Tiny Record Player is about 1½" square, or 8 times tinier than an LP record.**

RECORD

With Color 1, CO 8 sts onto 3 needles and join in a round.

Rnd 1: [Kfb] 8 times (16 sts).

Switch to Black.

Rnd 2: Knit.

Before beginning Round 3, slip the first st, and shift the beginning of the round 1 st over so that the slipped st is now the last st in the round. (This will make the color change look smoother in the finished piece.)

Rnd 3: [Kfb, k1] 8 times (24 sts).

Rnd 4: Knit.

Rnd 5: [Kfb, k2] 8 times (32 sts).

Rnd 6: Knit.

BO all sts loosely, and thread the tail end through the first bound-off st to make a smooth outside edge (**A**, below).

A After binding off the stitches on the Record, thread the tail end through the first bound-off stitch to give the piece a smooth edge.

BASE *(worked back to front)*

With Color 2, CO 32 sts onto 3 needles and join in a round.

Knit 22 rounds.

Divide sts evenly onto 2 needles, and BO using kitchener stitch.

Stuff fully without overstuffing, and close up the cast-on edge using mattress stitch.

ARM

With Color 3, CO 3 sts onto one needle. Work as an I-cord for 15 rows, then break the yarn and draw it tightly through the sts using a tapestry needle.

With the end still threaded through the needle, bend the tip of piece over at a 90-degree angle, and stitch it in place as you weave in the end **B**, below).

B After pulling the loose end through the last stitches in the arm, bend the tip at a 90-degree angle, and thread the end back through the piece to sew in place.

FINISHING

Block the Record by dampening it and laying it flat to dry.

Once the Record is dry, with Black, embroider eyes onto the Color 1 section using one small st for each, spaced about 3 sts apart.

Embroider eyes onto the front of the Base using 2 sts for each across one knitted st, spaced about 5 sts apart.

Attach the Record to the base using secure but not too-tight sts.

Attach the Arm to the Base.

With Color 3, embroider buttons spaced 2 sts apart. Go back over the embroidered sts once more to make them thicker.

Weave in loose ends.

Tiny Telephone

This one won't take messages, or look up a phone number, or find you directions. What does she look like, your secretary?

SPECIAL TECHNIQUES
Picking up stitches (page 20)
Kitchener stitch (page 140)
Back stitch (page 27)

YARN
Fingering-weight yarn in 2 colors and black
Sample made with Koigu Premium Merino
(1/super fine; 100% wool; 1¾ oz/50g, 170 yd/155m)
Main Color (MC): 1102

Contrasting Color (CC): 0000
Black: 2400

OTHER SUPPLIES
Set of size 1 U.S. (2.25mm) double-pointed needles
Stitch marker
Small tapestry needle
Stuffing

Tiny Telephone is about 1½" wide, or 5 times tinier than a Princess Phone.

BASE

With MC, CO 12 sts onto one needle to work straight.

Beginning with a purl row, work 12 rows in St st.

Instead of turning for the next purl row, rotate the piece 90 degrees clockwise, and pick up and knit 9 sts along the side of the piece with a second needle (right). With a third needle, pick up and knit 10 sts from the cast-on edge. With a fourth needle, pick up and knit 9 sts along the remaining side.

Distribute sts onto 3 needles, and place a marker. You will continue to knit these 40 sts in the round.

Rnd 1: Knit.
Rnd 2: {K2tog, k8, [k2tog] twice, k4, k2tog} twice (32 sts).
Rnd 3: Knit.

After finishing the flat section, turn the piece, and pick up and knit stitches around the other 3 sides of the piece. You will then distribute the stitches onto 3 needles before continuing to knit in a round to shape the base of the telephone.

Rnd 4: {K2tog, k6, [k2tog] twice, k2, k2tog} twice (24 sts).
Rnd 5: Knit.
Rnd 6: {K2tog, k4, [k2tog] 3 times} twice (16 sts).
Rnd 7: K15, remove marker.

Place the last st from the previous round next to the first st in the round, so that it becomes the first st and the other sts are shifted over by one. Stuff the piece.

Divide sts evenly onto 2 needles, and BO using kitchener stitch.

HANDSET

With MC, CO 4 sts onto one needle.

Rnd 1 (work as I-cord): [Kfb] 4 times (8 sts).

Distribute the sts onto 3 needles to continue to work in a round.

Rnd 2: [Kfb] 8 times (16 sts).

Rnds 3 and 4: Knit.

Rnd 5: [K2tog] 8 times (8 sts).

Insert a small amount of stuffing into the piece.

Rnd 6: [K2tog] 4 times (4 sts).

Place the sts onto one needle to continue to work as I-cord.

Rnds 7–16: Knit 10 rounds of I-cord.

Rnd 17 (work as I-cord): [Kfb] 4 times (8 sts).

Distribute the sts onto 3 needles to continue to work in a round.

Rnd 18: [Kfb] 8 times (16 sts).

Rnds 19–21: Knit.

Rnd 22: [K2tog] 8 times (8 sts).

Insert a small amount of stuffing into the end section of the piece.

Break the yarn and draw it tightly through the sts with a tapestry needle.

DIAL

With CC, CO 8 sts onto 3 needles and join in a round.

Rnd 1: [Kfb] 8 times (16 sts).

BO all sts loosely.

CORD

With CC, CO 2 sts onto one needle, and knit an I-cord until the piece is about 3" long.

BO all sts.

FINISHING

Place the Handset on top of the Base, and stitch in place.

Attach one end of the Cord to the back of the Base with a few sts, then twist the Cord tightly, so that it kinks up, before attaching the other end to the Handset.

Place the Dial onto the front side of the Base, and attach using back stitch.

With Black, embroider eyes onto the Base between the Handset and the Dial, with 2 small sts for each, spaced 3 sts apart.

Weave in loose ends.

Display Ad Page 373
01 E Admiral Pl
N 2234 W Houston
251 0220

er smart shoppers do.
pp in the AT&T
es, before you start out
You will be doing your
ve energy and you will
lot of time and money.

Joseph L 6139 E 91
Pryor Dental Center 1909 S Elliott
Rains G K 6 S Rowe

Shopping is as simple as
if you shop in the
AT&T Yellow Page

Tiny Naturals

Tiny Cacti

They're thinking somebody needs a hug!

YARN

Fingering-weight yarn in green, white, and black
Samples made with Koigu Premium Merino
(1/super fine; 100% wool; 1¾ oz/50g, 170 yd/155m)
Green (body): 2132
White (spikes): 0000
Black: 2400

OTHER SUPPLIES

Set of size 1 U.S. (2.25mm) double-pointed needles
Small tapestry needle
Small crochet hook (size B U.S. [2.25mm])
Stuffing

The taller Tiny Cactus is about 1½" tall, or 600 times tinier than the tallest saguaro.

BODY

With Green, CO 4 sts onto one needle.

Rnd 1 (work as I-cord): [Kfb] 4 times (8 sts).

Distribute the sts onto 3 needles and join in a round.

Rnd 2: [Kfb] 8 times (16 sts).

Rnd 3: Knit.

Rnd 4: [Kfb, k3] 4 times (20 sts).

Rnd 5: [K1, p1] to end.

Work 11 more rounds as established, in k1, p1 rib pattern.

Note: To make the taller cactus, work 6 extra rounds of the rib pattern.

Last round: [P2tog] to end (10 sts).

Turn the piece inside out, then stuff. Break the yarn and draw it tightly through the sts with a tapestry needle, threading through the sts counterclockwise, in the opposite direction from how you normally would.

ARMS *(make 4)*

With Green, CO 4 sts onto one needle.

Rnd 1 (work as I-cord): [Kfb] 4 times (8 sts).

Distribute the sts onto 3 needles and join in a round.

Rnd 2: [K1, p1] to end.

Work 5 more rounds as established, in k1, p1 rib pattern.

Stuff the piece, then break the yarn and draw it tightly through the sts with a tapestry needle.

Make 2 more Arms.

Make the fourth arm the same as the first but with one extra round of rib pattern to make it longer.

FINISHING

With Black, embroider eyes onto knit sts in the ribbing, using 3 sts per eye.

Attach the Arms to the sides of the Body at upward angle using a few sts.

For spikes, cut 5–7 approximately 5"-long strands of White. Fold each strand in half and weave it under a stitch on the Cactus using a crochet hook. Slip the ends of the yarn through the resulting loop and pull to tighten. Trim to short lengths.

Weave in loose ends.

Tiny Rainbow

She thinks she's pretty clever just because she's an optical illusion.

SPECIAL TECHNIQUES
Mattress stitch (page 24)

YARN
Fingering-weight yarn in blue, yellow, red, and black
Sample made with Koigu Premium Merino (1/super fine; 100% wool; 1¾ oz/50g, 170 yd/155m)
Blue: 2130
Yellow: 2100
Red: 2220
Black: 2400

OTHER SUPPLIES
Set of size 1 U.S. (2.25mm) double-pointed needles
Tapestry needle
Stuffing

Tiny Rainbow is about 1¼" tall and 2¼" wide, or 8 times tinier than a Rainbow Brite doll from 1983.

Note: Depending on your gauge, the length of your pieces may vary. Check lengths as noted in the pattern.

RAINBOW

With Blue, CO 6 sts onto 3 needles, leaving a long tail for seaming, and join in a round.

Rnd 1: [Kfb, k1] 3 times (9 sts).

Knit in a round until the piece measures about 1¼" long, stuffing lightly as you go. Break the yarn and draw it tightly through the sts with a tapestry needle.

Make a yellow piece in the same way, knitting until it measures about 2¼". Leave a long tail of yarn. After stuffing and before closing up the end, curve the yellow piece around the blue, with the blue piece folded in half. If the ends of the tubes don't line up, make the yellow piece longer until they do.

Make a red piece, knitting until it measures about 3½" long. Leave a long tail of yarn. Again, check the length by curving the red piece around the yellow and blue to check that the ends line up.

FINISHING

Line up the blue and yellow pieces, and curve them together so that the ends meet. With a tapestry needle, use the long tail you left on the yellow piece to sew the 2 pieces together using mattress stitch, inserting your needle under 2 sts on the blue for every 3 sts on the yellow (above, right).

Once the yellow and blue pieces are attached, curve the red piece around the yellow, and attach the red to the yellow in the same way that you attached the yellow to the blue.

Curve the blue and yellow pieces together, and sew them together using a tapestry needle and mattress stitch, inserting your needle under 2 stitches on the blue piece for every 3 stitches on the yellow.

Lightly squeeze the rainbow so that the blue piece is folded in half, and with the long tail that you left on it, sew the 2 halves together with a few sts. With Black and a tapestry needle, embroider eyes onto the yellow piece, with 3 vertical sts per eye, spaced about 5 sts apart.

Weave in loose ends.

Tiny Forest

It can't see itself for the trees!

SPECIAL TECHNIQUES
Mattress stitch (page 24)

YARN
Fingering-weight yarn in 3 colors and black
Sample made with Knit Picks Palette
(1/super fine; 100% wool; 1¾ oz/50g, 231 yd/211m)
Color 1 (grass): 24585 (Grass)

Color 2 (trunk): 24562 (Bison)
Color 3 (tree top): 24257 (Edamame)
Black: 23729

OTHER SUPPLIES
Set of size 1 U.S. (2.25mm) double-pointed needles
Small tapestry needle
Stuffing

> **Tiny Forest is about ¾" tall and 2½" wide, or 30 times tinier than Forest Whitaker.**

GRASS

With Color 1, CO 21 sts onto one needle to work straight.

Row 1: [K1, p1] to last st, k1.

Row 2: Work same as Row 1.

Work as established for 20 more rows.

BO all sts as established.

TREE (make 17, or as many as you like)

With Color 2, CO 4 sts onto one needle.

Knit 2 rows of I-cord.

Switch to Color 3.

Rnd 3 (work as I-cord): [Kfb] 4 times (8 sts).

Distribute the sts onto 3 needles and join in a round.

Rnd 4: [Kfb, k1] 4 times (12 sts).

Rnds 5–7: Knit.

Rnd 8: [K2tog, k1] 4 times (8 sts).

Rnd 9: Knit.

Insert a small amount of stuffing into the piece.

Rnd 10: [K2tog] 4 times (4 sts).

Break the yarn and draw it tightly through the sts with a tapestry needle.

Note: To make trees of varying height, knit 1 or 2 extra rounds of Color 2 before switching to Color 3.

FINISHING

Place one Tree close to the cast-on edge of the Grass, at the center, and attach the cast-on edge to the Grass using mattress stitch.

Attach 2 more Trees in line with the first, midway between the first and the side edge of the Grass.

Attach a second row of 4 Trees, staggered behind the first row.

The trees are attached to the grass in 5 staggered rows.

Attach 3 more rows in this way, staggering each row (above). Once the Trees are attached, embroider eyes with Black at the widest part of a Tree, with 2 small sts for each, spaced about 2 sts apart.

Weave in loose ends.

Tiny Volcano

He's sad because all of the villagers are running away. But also happy because now he can have fun destroying their village.

YARN

Fingering-weight yarn in brown, variegated red, and black
Sample made with Koigu Premium Merino (1/super fine; 100% wool; 1¾ oz/50g, 170 yd/155m)
Brown (volcano): 2395
Red (lava): P803
Black: 2400

OTHER SUPPLIES

Set of size 1 U.S. (2.25mm) double-pointed needles
Small tapestry needle
Stuffing

> Tiny Volcano is about 1¼" tall (not including lava), or 52 thousand times tinier than Iceland's Eyjafjallajökull.

VOLCANO

With Brown, CO 4 sts onto one needle.

Rnd 1 (work as I-cord): [Kfb] 4 times (8 sts).

Distribute the sts onto 3 needles and join in a round.

Rnd 2: [Kfb] 8 times (16 sts).

Rnd 3: Knit.

Rnd 4: [Kfb, k1] 8 times (24 sts).

Rnd 5: Knit.

Rnd 6: [Kfb, k2] 8 times (32 sts).

Rnds 7–10: Knit (4 rounds).

Rnd 11: [K2tog, k6] 4 times (28 sts).

Rnd 12: Knit.

Rnd 13: [K2tog, k5] 4 times (24 sts).

Rnd 14: Knit.

Rnd 15: [K2tog, k4] 4 times (20 sts).

Rnd 16: Knit.

Rnd 17: [K2tog, k3] 4 times (16 sts).

Rnd 18: Knit.

Rnd 19: [K2tog, k2] 4 times (12 sts).

Rnd 20: Knit.

BO all sts.

FINISHING

With Black, embroider eyes onto the Volcano with 3 sts for each, placed about 8 sts from the bound-off edge and spaced 3 sts apart.

For lava, cut 5 approximately 6"-long strands of Red. Tie them together in a knot in the middle (above, right).

For lava, cut 5 strands of red yarn, and tie them together in a knot in the middle.

Stuff the Volcano, then poke the knot of the lava inside the top. Stitch in place with loose sts of Brown if desired. Trim the lava to uneven lengths.

Weave in loose ends.

Small Saturn is about 1" in diameter, or 4 billion times tinier than the genuine Saturn.

Little Earth is about 1¼" in diameter, or 400 million times tinier than the actual Earth.

Mini Moon is about ¾" in diameter, or 300 million times tinier than the real Moon.

Tiny Planets

They may appear majestic, but the truth is they've spent the past two hundred years giggling at Uranus's name.

SPECIAL TECHNIQUES
Back stitch (page 27)

YARN
Fingering-weight yarn in 5 colors and black
Samples made with Koigu Premium Merino
(1/super fine; 100% wool; 1¾ oz/50g, 170 yd/155m)
Color 1 (Earth): 2130
Color 2 (continents): 1200
Color 3 (Saturn): P803
Color 4 (ring): 1171
Color 5 (Moon): 2392
Black: 2400

OTHER SUPPLIES
Set of size 1 U.S. (2.25mm) double-pointed
needles
Straight pins
Small tapestry needle
Stuffing

LITTLE EARTH
With Color 1, CO 6 sts onto 3 needles and join in a round.
Rnd 1: [Kfb] 6 times (12 sts).
Rnd 2: [Kfb, k1] 6 times (18 sts).
Rnd 3: Knit.
Rnd 4: [Kfb, k2] 6 times (24 sts).
Rnds 5 and 6: Knit.
Rnd 7: [Kfb, k3] 6 times (30 sts).
Rnds 8 and 9: Knit.
Rnd 10: [Kfb, k4] 6 times (36 sts).
Rnds 11 and 12: Knit.
Rnd 13: [K2tog, k4] 6 times (30 sts).
Rnds 14 and 15: Knit.
Rnd 16: [K2tog, k3] 6 times (24 sts).
Rnds 17 and 18: Knit.
Rnd 19: [K2tog, k2] 6 times (18 sts).
Rnd 20: Knit.
  Stuff the piece.
Rnd 21: [K2tog, k1] 6 times (12 sts).

Break the yarn and draw it tightly through the sts with a tapestry needle.

Africa
With Color 2, CO 3 sts onto one needle to work straight.
Rows 1–3: Beginning with a purl row, work 3 rows in St st.
Row 4: K1, [kfb] twice (5 sts).
Row 5: Purl.
Row 6: K2, [kfb] twice, k1.
Rows 7–9: Work 3 rows in St st.
  BO all sts.

South and North America
With Color 2, CO 2 sts onto one needle to work straight.
Row 1: Purl.
Row 2: K1, kfb (3 sts).
Row 3: Purl.
Row 4: K1, kfb, k1 (4 sts).

Row 5: Purl.
Row 6: [Kfb] twice, k2 (6 sts).
Row 7: Purl.
Row 8: BO 4 sts, then knit 1 (2 sts).
Row 9: Purl.
Row 10: CO 4 sts using backward loop, then knit all sts (6 sts).
Row 11–14: Work 4 rows in St st.
Row 15 (WS): BO 4 sts, then p1 (2 sts).
Row 16: Knit.
  BO both sts.

Europe and Asia
With Color 2, CO 4 sts onto one needle to work straight.
Row 1: Purl.
Row 2: K1, [kfb] twice, k1 (6 sts).
Row 3: Purl.
Row 4: K1, kfb, k2, kfb, k1 (8 sts).
Row 5: Purl.
Row 6: K1, kfb, k4, kfb, k1 (10 sts).

Row 7: CO 2 sts using backward loop, then purl to end (12 sts).
Row 8: CO 2 sts using backward loop, then knit to end (14 sts).
Row 9: BO 4 sts, then purl to end (10 sts). BO all sts.

Australia

With Color 2, CO 3 sts onto one needle to work straight.
Row 1: Purl.
  Break the yarn, and place the sts onto a spare needle to work later.
  Make a second piece the same as first but without breaking the yarn. Place the pieces side by side onto one needle, with the working yarn attached to the rightmost st. You will join the 6 sts with the next row.
Row 1: K1, kfb, k2, kfb, k1 (8 sts).
Row 2: Purl.
Row 3: K1, k2tog, k2, k2tog, k1 (6 sts).
Row 4: P1, [p2tog] twice, p1 (4 sts).
  BO all sts.

Antarctica

With Color 2, CO 3 sts onto one needle to work straight.
Row 1: Purl.
Row 2: [Kfb] 3 times (6 sts).
Rows 3–5: Work 3 rows in St st.
Row 6: [K2tog] 3 times (3 sts).
  BO all sts.

FINISHING EARTH

Place the continents onto Earth and pin in place (above, right). Use the tail ends to stitch along the outside edges of the continents.

Embroider eyes on each continent with black yarn, using 2 sts for each eye.
  Embroider eyes onto the Earth, between the Americas and Europe/Africa, using 3–4 sts of Black for each, spaced 3 sts apart. Weave in the ends.

Arrange the continents on Earth, pin in place, and stitch with the tail ends, using a back stitch. (Earth is shown from the back side.)

SMALL SATURN

With Color 3, CO 6 sts onto 3 needles and join in a round.
Rnd 1: [Kfb] 6 times (12 sts).
Rnd 2: [Kfb, k1] 6 times (18 sts).
Rnd 3: Knit.
Rnd 4: [Kfb, k2] 6 times (24 sts).
Rnds 5 and 6: Knit.
Rnd 7: [Kfb, k3] 6 times (30 sts).
Rnds 8–10: Knit.
Rnd 11: [K2tog, k3] 6 times (24 sts).
Rnds 12 and 13: Knit.
Rnd 14: [K2tog, k2] 6 times (18 sts).
Rnd 15: Knit.
  Stuff the piece.
Rnd 16: [K2tog, k1] 6 times (12 sts).
  Break the yarn and draw it tightly through the sts with a tapestry needle.

Ring

With Color 4, CO 24 sts onto 3 needles and join in a round.

Knit 6 rounds.
BO all sts.

FINISHING SATURN

Flip the Ring inside out so the purl sts face out, and place it around Saturn. Stitch in place.
  Embroider eyes with 3 sts of Black for each, spaced 2 sts apart. Weave in the ends.

MINI MOON

With Color 5, CO 6 sts onto 3 needles and join in a round.
Rnd 1: [Kfb] 6 times (12 sts).
Rnd 2: [Kfb, k1] 6 times (18 sts).
Rnds 3 and 4: Knit.
Rnd 5: [Kfb, k2] 6 times (24 sts).
Rnds 6–8: Knit.
Rnd 9: [K2tog, k2] 6 times (18 sts).
Rnds 10 and 11: Knit.
  Stuff piece.
Rnd 12: [K2tog] 9 times (9 sts).
Rnd 13: Knit.
  Break the yarn, leaving a long tail, and draw it tightly through the sts with a tapestry needle.

FINISHING MOON

With the long tail still on the needle, weave the tail in and out of the Moon at various places, pulling tightly after each st to make craterlike indentations on the surface.
  Embroider eyes with 2 sts of Black for each, spaced about 2 sts apart. Weave in the ends.

Tiny Island

He can't wait to get his first castaway. He's going to name him Fred.

SPECIAL TECHNIQUES
Mattress stitch (page 24)

YARN
Fingering-weight yarn in 4 colors and black
Sample made with Koigu Premium Merino
(1/super fine; 100% wool; 1¾ oz/50g, 170 yd/155m)
Color 1 (water): p904
Color 2 (island): 2100

Color 3 (tree trunk): 1230
Color 4 (palm leaves): 1520
Black: 2400

OTHER SUPPLIES
Set of size 1 U.S. (2.25mm) double-pointed needles
Small tapestry needle
Stuffing

Tiny Island is about 2½" tall, or 6 times tinier than the average coconut.

WATER

With Color 1, CO 4 sts onto one needle to work straight.

Row 1 and all odd-numbered rows: Purl.

Row 2: [Kfb] 4 times (8 sts).

Row 4: K1, [kfb] twice, k to last 3 sts, [kfb] twice, k1 (12 sts).

Row 6: Work same as Row 4 (16 sts).

Row 8: K1, kfb, k to last 2 sts, kfb, k1 (18 sts).

Row 10: Work same as Row 8 (20 sts).

Row 12: Work same as Row 8 (22 sts).

Rows 14, 16, and 18: Knit.

Row 20: K1, k2tog, k to last 3 sts, k2tog, k1 (20 sts).

Row 22: Work same as Row 20 (18 sts).

Row 24: Work same as Row 20 (16 sts).

Row 26: K1, [k2tog] twice, k6, [k2tog] twice, k1 (12 sts).

Row 28: K1, [k2tog] twice, k2, [k2tog] twice, k1 (8 sts).

Row 30: [K2tog] 4 times (4 sts). BO on the purl side.

ISLAND

With Color 2, CO 8 sts onto 3 needles and join in a round.

Rnd 1: [Kfb] 8 times (16 sts).

Rnd 2 and all even-numbered rounds through Rnd 12: Knit.

Rnd 3: [Kfb, k1] 8 times (24 sts).

Rnd 5: [Kfb, k2] 8 times (32 sts).

Rnd 7: Knit.

Rnd 9: [K2tog, k2] 8 times (24 sts).

Rnd 11: [K2tog, k2] 6 times (18 sts).

Rnd 13: [K2tog, k1] 6 times (12 sts).

Stuff the piece fully, without overstuffing.

Rnd 14: [K2tog] 6 times (6 sts).

Break the yarn and draw it tightly through the sts with a tapestry needle.

TREE TRUNK

With Color 3, CO 4 sts onto one needle, and knit 10 rows of I-cord.

Break the yarn and draw it tightly through the sts with a tapestry needle.

LEAVES

With Color 4, CO 3 sts onto one needle.

Knit 5 rows of I-cord.

Next row: K1, yo, k2tog.

Knit 5 more rows of I-cord.

Break the yarn and draw it tightly through the sts with a tapestry needle.

Make a second I-cord (without a yarn over), knitting for 11 rounds. Break the yarn and draw it tightly through the sts with a tapestry needle.

With the yarn of the second I-cord still threaded on the tapestry needle, insert the second I-cord through the first, and pull it halfway through, to make 4 Leaves. Stitch in place.

FINISHING

Block the Water by dampening it and laying it out flat to dry.

Once the Water has dried, place the Island on top of the Water, with the bottom of the Island against the knit side of the Water. Sew the Island to the Water using mattress stitch, stitching just above the last increase round on the Island.

With Black, embroider eyes onto the Island, with 3–4 sts per eye, placed 4 sts from the top and spaced 4 sts apart.

Attach the center Leaves to the Trunk with a few small sts, then attach the Trunk to the Island, placed behind the eyes and a little off center on the Island.

Weave in loose ends.

Tiny Holidays

Tiny Hugs and Kisses

When these guys aren't in the mood for love, they're always up for tic-tac-toe.

SPECIAL TECHNIQUES
Mattress stitch (page 24)

YARN
Fingering-weight yarn in red, pink, and black
Samples made with Koigu Premium Merino
(1/super fine; 100% wool; 1¾ oz/50g, 170 yd/155m)
Red: 2220

Pink: 1102
Black: 2400

OTHER SUPPLIES
Set of size 1 U.S. (2.25mm)
double-pointed needles
Small tapestry needle
Stuffing

Tiny Hugs and Kisses are each about 1" tall, or about the same size as a peck on the cheek.

KISS (X) (make 2)

Half Kiss (Half X)
With Red, CO 6 sts onto 3 needles and join in a round.
Rnd 1: [Kfb] 6 times (12 sts).
  Knit 16 rounds.
  Stuff the piece.
Next rnd: [K2tog] 6 times (6 sts).
  Break the yarn and draw it tightly through the sts with a tapestry needle.

Quarter Kiss (Quarter X) (make 2)
With Red, CO 12 sts onto 3 needles, leaving a tail for seaming, and join in a round.
  Knit 6 rounds.
Next rnd: [K2tog] 6 times (6 sts).
  Break the yarn and draw it tightly through the sts with a tapestry needle.

FINISHING KISS

Stuff one Quarter X, and place the cast-on edge against the side of the Half X, in the middle. Attach the Quarter X to the Half X using mattress stitch, stitching in a circular shape that matches the circle of the cast-on edge.

  Repeat with the remaining Quarter X, making sure that the 2 Quarter Xs are angled straight out from each other.

  With Black, embroider eyes onto the middle of the Half X piece with 2 small sts for each, spaced about 2 sts apart. Weave in the ends.

HUG (O) (make 2)

With Pink, CO 12 sts onto 3 needles and join in a round.
Rnd 1: [Kfb, k2] 4 times (16 sts).
Rnd 2 and all even-numbered rounds: Knit.

Rnd 3: [Kfb, k1] 8 times (24 sts).
Rnd 5: [Kfb, k2] 8 times (32 sts).
Rnd 7: Knit.
Rnd 9: [K2tog, k2] 8 times (24 sts).
Rnd 11: [K2tog, k1] 8 times (16 sts).
Rnd 13: [K2tog, k2] 4 times (12 sts).
  BO all sts, leaving a tail for seaming.

FINISHING HUG

Sew together the cast-on and bound-off edges with mattress stitch, pulling tightly to hide the edges, and stuff the piece before closing up.

  With Black, embroider eyes with 2 small sts for each, placed midway down the decrease side of the O and spaced about 4 sts apart.

  Weave in the ends.

Tiny Ghosts

These guys are more likely to kill you with cuteness than scare you to death.

YARN
Fingering-weight yarn in white and black
Samples made with Knit Picks Palette
(1/super fine; 100% wool; 1¾ oz/50g,
231 yd/211m)
White: 23730 (Cream)
Black: 23729

OTHER SUPPLIES
Set of size 1 U.S. (2.25mm) double-pointed needles
Small tapestry needle
Stuffing

> **Tiny Ghost is about ¾" tall, or 1,000 times less scary than a real ghost.**

BODY
With White, CO 36 sts onto 3
needles and join in a round.
Rnd 1: [K2tog, k1] 12 times (24 sts).
Rnd 2: [K2tog, k2] 6 times (18 sts).
Rnds 3–11: Knit (9 rnds).
Rnd 12: [K2tog, k1] 6 times (12 sts).
Rnd 13: [K2tog] 6 times (6 sts).

Break the yarn and draw it tightly through the sts with a tapestry needle.

EYES
With Black, embroider the eyes with 2 small sts for each, spaced about 4 sts from the top of the piece and spaced 3 sts apart.

ARMS
With White, CO 2 sts onto one needle.

Knit 12 rows of I-cord, then break the yarn and draw it tightly through the sts with a tapestry needle. With the end still threaded on the tapestry needle, insert the I-cord through the Body, going in and coming out at about 2 sts below and just to the outside of the eyes. Pull the I-cord halfway through the Body, leaving an even amount on each side. Weave the loose ends back through the Arms and Body.

FINISHING
Weave in loose ends.

Tiny Firecracker

He harbors a secret fear that he's a dud.

YARN

Fingering-weight yarn in red, blue, white, yellow, orange, and black

Sample made with Knit Picks Palette (1/super fine; 100% wool; 1¾ oz/50g, 231 yd/211m)

Red: 24553 (Serrano)
Blue: 24583 (Cyan)
White: 23730 (Cream)
Yellow: 24558 (Custard)
Orange: 24554 (Orange)
Black: 23729

OTHER SUPPLIES

Set of size 1 U.S. (2.25mm) double-pointed needles
Small tapestry needle
Stuffing

Tiny Firecracker is about 2" long, or pretty much the actual size of a Black Cat.

TUBE

With Red, CO 4 sts onto one needle.

Rnd 1 (work as I-cord): [Kfb] 4 times (8 sts).

Distribute the sts onto 3 needles and join in a round.

Rnd 2: [Kfb] 8 times (16 sts).

Rnd 3: Knit.

Switch to Blue, and knit 3 rounds.

Switch to Red, and knit 3 rounds.

Continue to alternate 3 rounds each of Red and Blue, until you have knit 3 stripes of Blue.

Switch to Red, and knit 2 rounds. Stuff the piece.

Next rnd: [K2tog] 8 times (8 sts).

Knit one more round, then break the yarn and draw it tightly through the sts with a tapestry needle.

FUSE

With White, CO 3 sts onto one needle.

Knit I-cord until approximately 1" long (or make it longer if using thicker yarn), then break the yarn and draw it tightly through the sts with a tapestry needle.

With the end still threaded on the tapestry needle, insert the end of the Fuse into the hole at the gathered sts on the Tube. Stitch in place.

FINISHING

With Black, embroider eyes with 2 small sts on 2 inside stripes of Red.

Cut 2 strands each of Yellow and Orange, and tie them together in a knot.

Tack the Yellow and Orange knotted strands onto the end of the Fuse, then trim the strands of yarn and fray with scissors.

Weave in loose ends.

Tiny Easter Bunny

While his bigger cousin brings the candy, this little rabbit just tests it for you.

SPECIAL TECHNIQUES
Picking up stitches (page 20)

YARN
Fingering-weight yarn in 2 colors and black
Sample made with Koigu Premium Merino
(1/super fine; 100% wool; 1¾ oz/50g, 170 yd/155m)
Color 1 (body): 1150.5

Color 2 (nose and tail): 1171
Black: 2400

OTHER SUPPLIES
Set of size 1 U.S. (2.25mm) double-pointed needles
Small tapestry needle
Stuffing

> Tiny Easter Bunny is about 1½" tall, or 50 times tinier than the imaginary rabbit in *Harvey*.

BODY *(worked bottom to top)*
With Color 1, CO 4 sts onto one needle.

Rnd 1 (work as I-cord): [Kfb] 4 times (8 sts).

Distribute the sts onto 3 needles and join in a round.

Rnd 2: [Kfb] 8 times (16 sts).

Rnds 3–5: Knit.

Rnd 6: [Kfb, k3] 4 times (20 sts).

Rnds 7–9: Knit.

Rnd 10: [Kfb, k4] 4 times (24 sts).

Rnds 11–14: Knit.

Rnd 15: [K2tog, k2] 6 times (18 sts).

Rnd 16: Knit.

Rnd 17: [K2tog, k1] 6 times (12 sts).

Stuff the piece.

Rnd 18: [K2tog] 6 times

Break the yarn and draw it tightly through the sts with a tapestry needle.

FEATURES
With Color 2, embroider a nose with 2 small sts placed about 5 sts from the top of the head.

With Black, embroider eyes using 2 small sts for each, placed about 4 sts from the top of the head, and spaced about 4 sts apart, on each side of the nose.

EARS *(make 2)*
Face the Body toward you, and with Color 1, pick up and knit 4 sts at the top of the head, with the innermost st at the top gathered sts (, above, right).

Ⓐ To begin making an ear, face the Body toward you, and pick up and knit 4 stitches at the top of the head, with the innermost stitch at the top gathered stitches.

Rnd 1 (work as I-cord): K1, [kfb] twice, k1 (6 sts).

Distribute the sts onto 3 needles, then knit 5 rounds.

Break the yarn and draw it tightly through the sts with a tapestry needle (without stuffing the piece).

Make a second ear the same way.

ARMS

With Color 1, CO 2 sts onto one needle. Knit 19 rows of I-cord, then break the yarn and draw it tightly through the sts with a tapestry needle.

With the end still threaded on the tapestry needle, insert the I-cord through the sides of the Body, going in and coming out at about 5 sts below the ears. Pull the I-cord halfway through the Body, leaving an even amount on each side. Weave the loose ends back through the I-cord and Body.

FEET (make 2)

Turn the Body upside down, and with Color 1, pick up and knit 4 sts out to the side at the second increase round on the Body, with the outermost st aligned with an arm (**B**, above, right).

B To begin making a foot, turn the Body upside down, and pick up and knit 4 stitches at the second increase round on the Body, with the outermost stitch aligned with an arm.

Knit 4 rows of I-cord, then break the yarn and draw it tightly through the sts with a tapestry needle (without stuffing the piece).

FINISHING

With Color 2, embroider a tail by horizontally wrapping 2 sts at the middle of the Bunny's back side 6–8 times (**C**, below).

C To embroider the tail onto the back side of the bunny, wrap 2 knitted stitches horizontally 6–8 times with Color 2.

Weave in loose ends.

Tiny Reindeer

They want everyone to be bad this year so they don't have so many presents to lug around.

SPECIAL TECHNIQUES
Picking up stitches (page 20)

YARN
Fingering-weight yarn in 3 colors and black
Samples made with Knit Picks Palette
(1/super fine; 100% wool; 1¾ oz/50g, 231 yd/211m)
Color 1 (body): 24240 (Doe)
Color 2 (antlers and hooves): 24562 (Bison)
Color 3 (Rudolf's nose): 24567 (Rouge)
Black: 23729

OTHER SUPPLIES
Set of size 1 U.S. (2.25mm) double-pointed needles
Small tapestry needle
Stuffing

Tiny Reindeer is about 2" long, or 40 times tinier than a typical flightless reindeer.

BODY *(worked back to front)*
With Color 1, CO 6 sts onto 3 needles and join in a round.
Rnd 1: [Kfb] 6 times (12 sts).
Rnd 2: Knit.
Rnd 3: [Kfb, k1] 6 times (18 sts).
Rnd 4: Knit.
Rnd 5: K2tog, yo, k to last 2 sts, yo, k2tog (18 sts).
Rnd 6: [Kfb, k2] 6 times (24 sts).
Rnds 7–9: Knit.
Rnd 10: [K2tog, k2] 6 times (18 sts).
Rnd 11: K2tog, yo, k to last 2 sts, yo, k2tog (18 sts).
Rnd 12: [K2tog, k1] 6 times (12 sts).
Rnd 13: [Kfb, k1] 6 times (18 sts).
Rnd 14: Knit.
Rnd 15: [Kfb, k2] 6 times (24 sts).
Rnd 16: Knit.
Rnd 17: K10, yo, [k2tog] twice, yo, k10 (24 sts).
Rnd 18: [K2tog, k2] 6 times (18 sts).
Rnd 19: Knit.
Rnd 20: [K2tog, k1] 6 times (12 sts).
Rnd 21: Knit.
  Stuff the piece.
Rnd 22: [K2tog] 6 times (6 sts).
  Break the yarn and draw it tightly through the sts with a tapestry needle.

LONG ANTLER
With Color 2, CO 3 sts onto one needle.
  Knit 18 rows of I-cord.
  Break the yarn and draw it tightly through the sts with a tapestry needle.
  With the end still on the tapestry needle, thread the I-cord through the yarn-over holes at the top of the head. Pull the I-cord halfway through, leaving an even amount on each side.
  Weave in the ends.

SHORT ANTLER (make 2)

With Color 2, CO 2 sts onto one needle.

Knit 10 rows of I-cord.

Break the yarn and draw it tightly through the sts with a tapestry needle.

With the end still on the tapestry needle, thread the I-cord through one side of the Long Antler piece, midway up. Pull the I-cord halfway through.

Weave in the ends.

LEGS (make 2)

With Color 2, CO 3 sts onto one needle.

Knit 1 row of I-cord.

Switch to Color 1.

Knit 10 rows of I-cord.

Switch to Color 2.

Knit 2 rows of I-cord.

Break the yarn and draw it tightly through the sts with a tapestry needle.

With the end still on the tapestry needle, insert the I-cord from back to front through the yarn-over holes on the bottom of the Body. Pull the I-cord halfway through to form one front and one back Leg. Repeat with the remaining I-cord Legs piece. Weave in the ends.

TAIL

With Color 1, pick up and knit 3 sts at the rear of the Body, just above the cast-on sts.

Knit 2 rows of I-cord, then break the yarn and draw it tightly through the sts with a tapestry needle.

With the end still on the tapestry needle, tack the top of the tail down with a few small sts.

FINISHING

With Black, embroider eyes with 2 sts, placed just in front of each antler.

With Color 2 (or with Color 3 for Rudolf), embroider a nose with 4 sts at the gathered sts.

Weave in loose ends.

Tiny Christmas Tree

Tiny Christmas Tree wishes you a merry Christmas! He also wishes he hadn't been chopped down, but hey, you can't have everything.

SPECIAL TECHNIQUES
Back stitch (page 27)

YARN
Fingering-weight yarn in green, yellow, brown, red, blue, and black
Sample made with Koigu Premium Merino (1/super fine; 100% wool; 1¾ oz/50g, 170 yd/155m)
Green: 1520
Yellow: 2100
Brown: 2395
Red: 2220
Blue: 2130
Black: 2400

OTHER SUPPLIES
Set of size 1 US (2.25mm) double-pointed needles
Small tapestry needle
Stuffing

> Tiny Christmas Tree is about 1¼" tall, or 60 times tinier than a Douglas Fir from a tree farm.

TREE

With Green, CO 20 sts onto 3 needles, leaving a tail for seaming, and join in a round.

Rnds 1 and 2: Knit.
Rnd 3: K2tog, k6, [k2tog] twice, k6, k2tog (16 sts).
Rnd 4: Purl.
Rnds 5 and 6: Knit.
Rnd 7: K2tog, k4, [k2tog] twice, k4, k2tog (12 sts).
Rnd 8: Purl.
Rnds 9 and 10: Knit.
Rnd 11: K2tog, k2, [k2tog] twice, k2, k2tog (8 sts).
Rnd 12: Purl.
Rnd 13: Knit.
 Switch to Yellow.
Rnd 14: [K2tog] 4 times (4 sts).
Rnd 15: [Kfb] 4 times (8 sts).

Rnd 16: Knit.
 Break the yarn and draw it tightly through the sts with a tapestry needle.

TRUNK

With Brown, CO 6 sts onto 3 needles and join in a round.

 Knit 4 rounds.
 Break the yarn and draw it tightly through the sts with a tapestry needle.

FINISHING

Lightly stuff the Tree, and place the tip of the cast-on end of the Trunk inside the open edge of the Tree.

 Pinch the Tree flat along the decrease sts, and sew the bottom closed using a back stitch, stitching the Trunk in place at the same time (above, right).

Place the tip of the Trunk inside the bottom of the Tree, then pinch the bottom flat, and sew it together using a back stitch, while also stitching the Trunk in place.

With Black, embroider eyes onto the middle (knit area) of the Tree, with 2 small sts for each, spaced 2 sts apart.

 With Red and Blue, embroider ornaments with 2 small sts for each—these sts should be smaller and tighter than the eyes.

 Weave in loose ends.

Tiny Possibilities

I think we can all agree that Tinys are devastatingly cute on their own and need no justification for their existence, but at the back of your mind you might still be wondering, "Yes, but what can I *do* with them?" The answer is: plenty!

For most of these projects, the necessary attachments can be purchased at any craft store. Remember when inserting a jump ring into a Tiny to make sure you insert it so the little guy will face forward when dangling. The direction will differ depending on the attachment you are using and the way it needs to hang.

Wear Them!

Tiny Earrings

To make your Tinys dangle, attach them to an earring hook with a jump ring. These flirty XOXO earrings are a must-wear for your birthday, anniversary, or Valentine's Day (of course!).

Tiny Charm Bracelet

Decorate a purchased charm bracelet for your most charming friend. This mixed-theme version would be perfect for a hot-dog vendor who loves gardening and dreams of being an astronaut someday.

Carry Them!

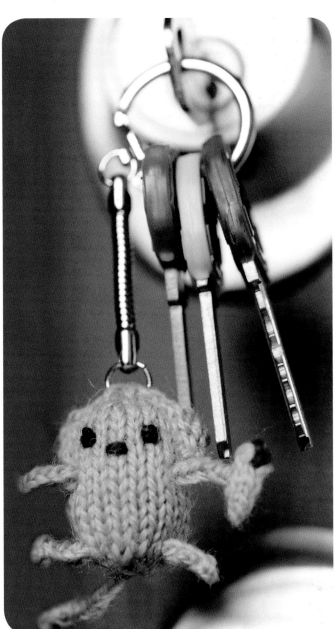

Tiny Keychain

The more discreet lover of Tinys can carry their knitted friend tucked away in a pocket. Just insert a jump ring under a few stitches at the top of the little guy, and attach to a keychain.

Tiny Pins

Customize a bag or jacket with your favorites. Use matching yarn and a small tapestry needle to sew each Tiny to a pin back.

Display Them!

Tiny Magnets

Forget a remodeling—outfit your kitchen with knitted toys! After stuffing, insert a magnet between the stuffing and the back of the piece. After closing up, move the magnet around a bit until it's in just the right spot.

Tiny Office Mates

This one is simple—everyone with a workspace can use a few silly little somethings to keep up morale. The fun part is matching the Tinys to the personalities of your office mates.

Give Them!

Tiny Gift Toppers

Add a cute flourish to a gift by attaching Tinys to a bow with matching yarn. Now you just have to figure out what to put inside. (I suggest more Tinys!)

Tiny Ornaments

Wow your family with personalized Christmas ornaments: Loop a piece of yarn through the top of a Tiny and attach it to an ornament hook or an unbent paper clip. One Tiny ornament can fit right inside the envelope with a holiday card.

Knitting Essentials

Basic Stitches

I recommend starting out by learning to knit with two needles, then switching to double-pointed needles (see page 14) once you feel comfortable with the basics.

CASTING ON (CO)

The most common way to start a knitting project is with a long-tail cast-on. Use it unless the directions specify otherwise.

Based on the number of stitches to cast on, estimate how much of a tail you will need.

1 Make a slip knot with the yarn, slide the needle through the knot, and tighten. This will become the first stitch in the cast-on.

2 Grasp both yarn ends in your left hand, with the yarn attached to the ball around the outside of your thumb and the tail around the outside of your forefinger.

3 With the needle in your right hand, insert the tip of the needle under the outer side of the yarn on your thumb, then dip it over and around the inner side of the yarn on your finger.

4 Let the yarn slip off your thumb, and pull outward slightly on the stitch you just made to tighten the loop on the needle.

Repeat Steps 2–4, trying to cast on all your stitches with the same tension, until you have the required number of stitches on your needle.

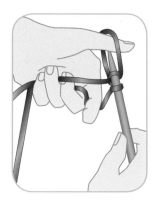

THE KNIT STITCH (K)

The knit stitch is the most basic stitch.

1 Hold the needle with the stitches in your left hand, with the yarn attached to the rightmost stitch. Hold the empty needle in your right hand. (In circular knitting, the attached yarn will be on a different needle—see Using Double-Pointed Needles on page 14.) Insert the tip of the right needle under the front of the first stitch on the left needle.

2 Wrap the yarn around the tip of the needle in your right hand, wrapping on top of the needle, from left to right.

3 Pull the right needle back out through the stitch on the left needle, pulling the wrapped yarn out with it.

4 Slip the stitch off the left needle. You now have a new stitch on the right needle.

Repeat Steps 1–4 as many times as indicated in the pattern, or until you have transferred all the stitches from the left needle to the right.

When you come to the end of the row:

If you are knitting a flat piece with 2 needles, switch the right needle to your left hand and flip it around for the next row.

If you are knitting with double-pointed needles, keep the right needle in the same position and move on to knit from the next needle that follows in the round.

THE PURL STITCH (P)

The purl stitch is the reverse of the knit stitch—it happens automatically on the reverse side of knitted stitches. When knitting a flat piece, you flip the piece around to work purl stitches on the reverse side.

1 Insert the tip of the right needle under the front of the first stitch on the left needle, going in from the right side and coming out in front of the left needle. Wrap the yarn around the top of the needle, from right to left.

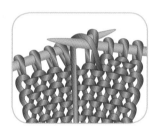

2 Pull the right needle back out through the stitch the left needle, pulling the wrapped yarn out with it.

3 As you pull the needle and yarn through, slip the stitch off the left needle.

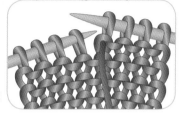

Repeat Steps 1–3 as many times as indicated in the pattern, or until you have transferred all of the stitches from the left needle to the right.

BINDING OFF (BO)

Most of the three-dimensional pieces in this book end with instructions to draw a loose end of yarn through the stitches to close off. For flat pieces, however, the usual finishing technique is to bind off stitches.

Knit the first 2 stitches in the row as you normally would.

Slip the left needle into the first stitch you knit, and pull it over the second stitch and completely off the needle. One stitch is bound off.

Knit the next stitch in the row, so that you again have 2 stitches on the right needle and repeat until there are no more stitches on the left needle and you are left with only one stitch on the right needle.

To finish off, break the yarn, slip the stitch off the needle, and slip the loose end through the stitch. Pull tightly to secure. Note: If a pattern calls for you to bind off on the purl side of a piece, you will bind off in the

same way as described above, except that you will purl all stitches instead of knitting them.

Increase and Decrease Stitches

You'll need increase and decrease stitches to knit more than a rectangle or a straight tube—like some curves!

KNIT THROUGH FRONT AND BACK OF A STITCH (KFB)

1 Knit a stitch just as you normally would, but without pulling the stitch off the left needle.

2 Knit into the same stitch again, this time inserting the tip of the right needle through the back leg of the stitch. Once you pull the right needle and yarn through, slip the left stitch off the needle.

This will increase the total number of stitches by 1.

KNIT 2 TOGETHER (K2TOG)

Insert the right needle under the first 2 stitches on the left needle. Wrap the yarn as you would normally do for a knit stitch, and slip both stitches off the left needle.

This will decrease the total number of stitches by 1.

PURL 2 TOGETHER (P2TOG)

Insert the tip of the right needle purlwise through the front of the first 2 stitches on the left needle. Wrap the yarn around, pull it through, and slip both stitches off the left needle.

This will decrease the total number of stitches by 1.

Beyond The Basics

I-CORD

An I-cord is a tiny tube of circular knitting made using two double-pointed needles.

Slide the stitches down the needle in your left hand so that the stitch without the yarn attached is on the right side. Knit the first stitch with the yarn that is connected to the last stitch, pulling the yarn around the back of the needle. Continue to knit to the end of the row.

When you reach the end of the row, instead of turning to work the other side, again slide the stitches down the needle and knit the first stitch with the yarn that is connected to the last stitch.

YARN OVER (YO)

Yarn over is an increase stitch that makes a small hole in your knitting.

1 Bring the yarn around in front of the needle in your right hand.

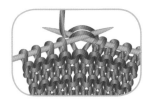

2 Knit the following stitch as you normally would, wrapping the yarn around the needle in the back.

PICKING UP STITCHES ON A FLAT PIECE

Picking up stitches along the side of a finished piece will allow you to knit in another direction, and in the case of toy knitting, it will help you to add another dimension to your knitting. (Most of the patterns in this book call for stitches to be picked up in the middle of a three-dimensional piece. See page 20 for this technique.) With the piece turned sideways, insert the tip of the needle under the first side stitch. Wrap the yarn around as you would for a knit stitch, and pull the yarn out through the stitch.

Repeat across the side of the piece, adjusting for the difference between the number of side stitches and the number of stitches to be picked up by skipping every fourth or fifth side stitch.

JOINING A NEW COLOR

To join a new color of yarn, tie the end of the working yarn and the beginning of the new color yarn together in a loose knot. Knit one stitch with the new yarn, then gently pull the knot tighter and closer to the back or the wrong side of the piece.

Use this technique when a pattern calls for you to switch to a new yarn color, and you won't be using the first color again (or not again for many rows).

As a no-knot alternative, you can twist the tail end of the old color once over the new color yarn after knitting the first stitch in the new color. Then, after knitting one row or round with the new color, pull the 2 tail ends tightly.

If you will use the first color again soon, as in a striped piece of alternating colors, do not cut the yarn, but instead carry the first color loosely up the side or back of the piece until you will use it again.

STRANDED COLOR KNITTING

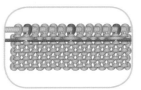

Stranded color knitting (or Fair Isle, as it's also known) is a method of carrying multiple strands of different colors of yarn along the back of a piece as you knit, incorporating the different colors in your stitches as you need them. There will often be a chart to refer to for the color changes.

You want to keep a consistent, relatively loose gauge, without pulling any stitches too tight, so the finished piece doesn't pucker.

As you knit, you can either hold the 2 strands of color in different hands, or you can simply drop the color that you're not working with at the moment (my preferred method). Wrap the colors of yarn around each other every few stitches to secure the yarn not being used.

Looking at the back of the piece, you should see the 2 strands of yarn, smooth and not puckered, across the entire length of a row.

KITCHENER STITCH

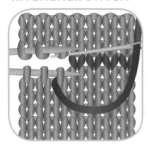

The kitchener stitch allows you to seam two pieces or sections of knitting together in an invisible way. The result is similar to the mattress stitch (see page 24), but it is more limited in its use.

Divide the live stitches onto 2 needles, with an even number of stitches on each needle. Hold the needles parallel to each other, with the working yarn attached to the rightmost stitch on the needle in back.

Cut the working yarn, leaving a long tail, and thread the tail onto a tapestry needle. Insert the tapestry needle purlwise (as if to purl) through the first (rightmost) stitch on the front needle, without slipping the stitch off the needle. Pull the tail through. Next, insert the tapestry needle knitwise through the first stitch on the back needle and pull it through, again without slipping the stitch off the needle. These 2 stitches set you up to begin the kitchener stitch pattern.

Now you will repeat the same pattern to finish off the seaming: knit, purl, purl, knit. Insert the tapestry needle knitwise through the first stitch on the front needle, and slip the stitch off the needle. Next, insert the tapestry needle purlwise through the following stitch on the front needle, without slipping the stitch off the needle.

Insert the tapestry needle purlwise through the first stitch on the back needle, and slip the stitch off the needle. Then, insert the tapestry needle knitwise through the following stitch on the back needle, without slipping the stitch off the needle.

Repeat these 4 stitches, 2 front and 2 back, until only one stitch remains on each needle. Insert the tapestry needle knitwise through the stitch on the front needle and slip it off, then insert the tapestry needle purlwise through the back needle and slip off.

PICKING UP A DROPPED STITCH

Dropped stitches happen to the best of us. If you notice

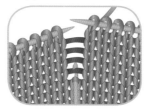

that your stitch count is off, you may have a "run" in your knitting, where one stitch has fallen off the needle, and a vertical row of stitches has unraveled along with it.

Instead of ripping out the entire piece and starting over, insert a crochet hook through the bottommost stitch that is still in place, then hook the bar that lies directly above it. Pull the bar through the stitch, then repeat for every bar above until you reach your topmost row of stitches. All fixed!

Yarn Weight System

YARN WEIGHT CATEGORIES	**0** LACE	**1** SUPER FINE	**2** FINE	**3** LIGHT	**4** MEDIUM	**5** BULKY	**6** SUPER BULKY
TYPES OF YARN IN CATEGORY	Fingering, 10-count crochet thread	Sock, fingering, baby	Sport, baby	DK, light worsted	Worsted, afghan, aran	Chunky, craft, rug	Bulky, roving
KNIT GAUGE RANGE *(in stockinette stitch to 4")*	33–40 sts	27–32 sts	23–26 sts	21–24 sts	16–20 sts	12–15 sts	6–11 sts
RECOMMENDED NEEDLE SIZES *(U.S./metric sizes)*	000–1 *(1.5–2.25mm)*	1–3 *(2.25–3.25mm)*	3–5 *(3.25–3.75mm)*	5–7 *(3.75–4.5mm)*	7–9 *(4.5–5.5mm)*	9–11 *(5.5–8mm)*	11 and larger *(8mm and larger)*

Adapted from the Standard Yarn Weight System
of the Craft Yarn Council of America.

Knitting Abbreviations

Here is a list of abbreviations used in the patterns in this book.

<	Less than
[]	Repeat actions in brackets number as many times as specified
approx	Approximately
BO	Bind off
CO	Cast on
est	Established
k	Knit
k2tog	Knit 2 stitches together
kfb	Knit through front and back of one stitch
kfbf	Knit into front of stitch, then knit into back of stitch, then into front again before slipping stitch off left needle (increases by 2 stitches)
p	Purl
p2tog	Purl 2 stitches together
rnd(s)	Round(s)
RS	Right side
st(s)	Stitch(es)
St st	Stockinette stitch (knit on right side, purl on wrong side)
WS	Wrong side
yo	Yarn over

Metric Conversion Chart

Inches to CM		CM to Inches			
$^1/_{16}$	0.16	1	$^3/_8$	26	10 $^1/_4$
$^1/_8$	0.32	2	$^3/_4$	27	10 $^5/_8$
$^3/_{16}$	0.48	3	1 $^1/_8$	28	11
$^1/_4$	0.64	4	1 $^5/_8$	29	11 $^3/_8$
$^5/_{16}$	0.79	5	2	30	11 $^7/_8$
$^3/_8$	0.95	6	2 $^3/_8$	31	12 $^1/_4$
$^7/_{16}$	1.11	7	2 $^1/_4$	32	12 $^5/_8$
$^1/_2$	1.27	8	3 $^1/_8$	33	13
$^9/_{16}$	1.43	9	3 $^1/_2$	34	13 $^3/_8$
$^5/_8$	1.59	10	4	35	13 $^3/_4$
$^{11}/_{16}$	1.75	11	4 $^3/_8$	36	14 $^1/_8$
$^3/_4$	1.91	12	4 $^3/_4$	37	14 $^5/_8$
$^{13}/_{16}$	2.06	13	5 $^1/_8$	38	15
$^7/_8$	2.22	14	5 $^1/_2$	39	15 $^3/_8$
$^{15}/_{16}$	2.38	15	5 $^7/_8$	40	15 $^3/_4$
1	2.54	16	6 $^1/_4$	41	16 $^1/_8$
2	5.08	17	6 $^3/_4$	42	16 $^1/_2$
3	7.65	18	7 $^1/_8$	43	16 $^7/_8$
4	10.16	19	7 $^1/_2$	44	17 $^1/_4$
5	12.70	20	7 $^7/_8$	45	17 $^3/_4$
6	15.24	21	8 $^1/_4$	46	18 $^1/_8$
7	17.78	22	8 $^5/_8$	47	18 $^1/_2$
8	20.32	23	9	48	18 $^7/_8$
9	22.66	24	9 $^1/_2$	49	19 $^1/_4$
10	25.40	25	9 $^7/_8$	50	19 $^5/_8$
11	27.94				
12	30.48				
13	33.02				
14	35.56				
15	38.10				
16	40.64				
17	43.18				
18	45.72				
19	48.26				
20	50.80				

Resources

Materials

YARN

Fingering-weight yarn for the patterns in this book is easy to find in yarn shops and craft stores. I used two brands. Koigu, which is a joy to knit with and comes in a variety of vibrant colors, is available at many local yarn stores. Knit Picks Palette yarn, which is available at affordable prices online in the United States, comes in more subtle colors and gives a nice fuzzy look to finished toys.

Koigu Wool Designs
www.koigu.com

Knit Picks
www.knitpicks.com

STUFFING

Dick Blick Art Materials
www.dickblick.com

Hobby Lobby
www.hobbylobby.com

Jo-Ann Fabric and Craft Stores
www.joann.com

Michaels
www.michaels.com

Online

There are a myriad of knitting tutorials, patterns, and communities online. Here are some of my favorite knitting-related websites.

Craft
www.craftzine.com
Web-based publication with patterns, tips, and craft news.

Etsy
www.etsy.com
Marketplace of crafters who sell their original handmade crafts, patterns, and vintage goods online.

KnittingHelp.com
www.knittinghelp.com
Website with videos demonstrating basic and advanced knitting techniques.

Knitty
www.knitty.com
Online knitting magazine with lots of fun patterns, including toys.

Mochimochi Land
www.mochimochiland.com
My website! You can find lots more knitted toy patterns here.

Ravelry
www.ravelry.com
An online knitting community and a great resource for patterns, yarns, and technical help.

Tiny Inspiration

If you love miniatures, check out what these very patient crafters are doing.

Bugknits
www.bugknits.com
Eye-popping miniature knitted garments from an artist who contributed to the costuming for the stop-motion animated film Coraline.

Do Little Design
www.etsy.com/shop/dolittledesign
Itty-bitty sewn and needle-felted creations.

MUFFA Miniatures
www.muffa-minis.blogspot.com
Insanely small crocheted animals by a talented microcrafter.

World's Smallest Post Service
www.leafcutterdesigns.com
The littlest letters imaginable hand-written with your custom message by a very steady hand.

Index

Page numbers in italics indicate projects.